A WORKING MODEL OF
THE FALL FROM GRACE

First published in 2019
by The Next Review
& Offord Road Books

Typeset by Offord Road Books
Printed in the UK by TJ International

ISBN 978–1–999–93042–4

1 3 5 7 9 10 8 6 4 2

A WORKING MODEL OF
THE FALL FROM GRACE

★

Essays & Poems
for David Harsent

DAVID HARSENT

Photograph by Simon Harsent © 2014

CONTENTS

MATTHEW HOLLIS

Foreword

It is said of Heraclitus that he spoke the words: It is impossible to step into the same river twice (a fragment known to scholars as B91). Or did he in fact say: On those who step into the same rivers different and different waters flow (B12)? Argument rages; our philosophers won't agree. Which idea is genuine, and which are we asked to consider? For the two fragments send us in differing directions. The first appears engaged with the thought that change is constant and that no moment may be revisited; the second seems concerned to tell us that the same moment is experienced differently by each person within it. Those are distinctive expressions: one about ceaseless flux, the other about relative experience.

It is the spring of 2019, and I'm finishing work with David Harsent on a new typescript, the sixth that I have been fortunate to see as his editor at Faber & Faber. And I'm wondering about the divergence of these two statements, because I have no doubt that the first fragment well describes the distinguished and ever-altering path of David's writing. His new typescript is unlike his last, which was unlike the one before it and the one before that; and so on, back to the beginning. Poems make common occurrences, as they do in all our writings, but David never steps into the same book twice. Each one engages us at different speeds, makes new demands of our eye and our breathing, provides us with a new measure of time. There is nothing forced about these renewals in production, nothing so deliberate as a solo singer changing their backing band; instead, it comes naturally to David's work, because each book arrives to him differently, or so I imagine. The incessancy of each one may express of the idea that every situation takes place in a moment that is altered from the last.

But what of the different and different waters from the second fragment: might it be said that we experience the same writing differently? No doubt we do. And yet readers find agreement on so many matters in literature that we must be sharing more than we know. Sometimes we say that there are such things as great poems or famous lines, and we put them in our literary front window. But David's readers are not distracted by the front window; they go deep into the house and take findings from the rafters or the staircase as intrinsic and valuable as anything that faces onto the street. Their haul is various and deep, and I have witnessed time and again how what they bring back electrifies them, for David's is a writing that serves to empower the writing of others. At such moments, it seems that readers have not merely had an experience that they like, it is as though they have found love. And it is with this spirit that the contributors to this volume generously guide us.

Whichever fragment best captures our imagination, each may bring light upon this poetry of incessant change and uncommon experience. But there's a third river fragment that I haven't yet mentioned, one that is sometimes thought of as the poor relation, no more than a paraphrase of the second, its more mysterious parent. In some ways it seems to me the most mysterious of all. It says this. Into the same rivers we step and we do not step, we are and we are not (B49a). What do we mean by that, we wonder? Perhaps we mean that in having the experience we change and are changed by it. And that wouldn't be far off what I'm hoping to say about David Harsent. Not far off at all.

Matthew Hollis is Poetry Editor at Faber & Faber

FIONA BENSON

Minotaur

for David Harsent

Descend again
to the beast
dumb housed
in the pitch dark

matrixed in
his sullen stall
of shit and offal,
humbles spooled

at the gore,
bull-stale,
maggot-crawl,
endless driven jism.

Listen as he dreams
his intolerable dream
of a word to speak –
a single word –

a name –
to ladder him up
into clean sea light
and meadow.

Put on his scab-
and-horsehair pelt,
his bit and bridle,
his spine's clubbed staples,

put on his clotted tongue.
He is my brother,
this half-and-half,
he is my monstrous heart.

Teach him now to sing.

JOHN CLEGG

Happy Harsent

No writer with a large enough corpus stays a pessimist. Robert Burton tried to write *The Anatomy of Melancholy*, which ended up being one of the most life-affirming books ever written – Keats and Johnson found it so – because it goes on so long; to be copious is to entail and affirm the world. J. H. Prynne wrote a book against language, and it might have been effective if he hadn't gone on to write three more on the same subject. The objects of reference swarmed against him, and by the end of *Streak~~~Willing~~~Entourage / 'Artesian'* we are rooting for language against the author. Just so with Celan: the late poems are well aware of the early ones, which have supposedly said everything that can be said; they pull pranks and make faces behind the poet's back. Just so with Ingeborg Bachmann: her anti-affirmation, about halfway through her *Collected Poems*, reaches a critical mass and wrenches her through the mirror, and after that, each thing she writes endorses the world and everything in it. If things didn't need endorsement, if the pessimist's case was true, why wouldn't she have stopped sooner?

And just so with David Harsent. If he'd stopped after *A Violent Country*, the poems in that volume would have been enough to secure a reputation as a pessimist. If, after saying of the dead 'Ignore them. / They are the earth's junk', he had followed his own advice, he might have ended up – like his early mentor Ian Hamilton – as the writer of a single, sublimely depressing book. But he can't ignore the dead, nor the rest of the earth's junk; junk which, in fact, becomes a preoccupation right up to the erased catalogues of *Legion*, in which it is his sole subject.

In the long poem 'Elsewhere' (from *Night*, 2011), Harsent finds himself following a dog (a 'brindled' dog – I looked up 'brindled', to see if it meant 'shaggy') through 'a tumbled scree // of bottles and cola cans and KFC / which puts me in mind of the time we climbed a tor . . .' – and the sentence trots off, following its own dog. The narrative of 'Elsewhere' is bleak, incredibly so; the scenery is bleak; but the experience of reading the poem, its rhythm, its impulse, is joyful. The earth's junk puts you in mind of more junk (cf. Paul Muldoon's poem on Nerval's suicide: 'which made me think // of something else, then something else again'). The ball, once it's started, keeps rolling, accumulating junk, more and more junk, like the spheres in *Katamari Damacy*. There's nothing for it but to quote at length: having come to the conclusion that he might have wasted his life, and still following the dog, he's propelled

> through alleys and backstreets (the dog in her element
> opening bin-bags to nuzzle the rich black mash),
> that takes me past car-lots and workshops, past greasy spoons,
> past walk-up and rack-rent,
> past casinos and clubs and shebeens, past Mr. Moon's
> Tattoo Shack, past day-for-night hotels, past cash-
> on-the-nail, past rat-runs and bargain bazaars, arcades,
>
> dives and dumps, cross-cuts, bootleg cabs,
> the house of correction and the house of jades,
> fast food portals, a patch of green, or what was once
> green, its litter of cans and condoms and needles, past
> the damaged, the derelict, the up-for-grabs,
> past flea-pits and burn-outs, no entry, no refunds,
> no-win-no-fee . . .

The dog might well be in her element; what's obvious is that Harsent is too, and the mood that's dragged him here ('a sense of pleasure / gone to waste') is a temporary funk – nobody could write as well as this if they didn't love the rat-runs and cross-cuts and flea-pits for their own sake, not to mention the language which forms these compounds so easily, with such casual energy and grandiloquence. (Incidentally, I wonder what a flea-pit is when it isn't a metaphor. Is it an armpit?)

I've heard that the problem with this sort of relish is that some people have to live permanently in the shebeens and flea-pits, and taking pleasure in them might restrain us from improving them. This is the same as the commonly raised objection to Harsent's violent grotesqueries: 'a shrapnel-wound pursing its lips and blowing a bubble' (from 'Snapshots', *Legion*) is vivid and surprising, but if we seek out our quota of vividity and surprise in descriptions of horrors – so the objection runs – we might become desensitised; the genuine shrapnel-wound, when it comes, might come as a disappointment.

I don't share this objection, nor do I quite know how to answer it. I don't think it will do to claim, as Patrick Davidson Roberts does, that Harsent doesn't deliberately go in search of these horrors. The introductory poem to *Night* refutes that quite adequately: 'There's a smell of scorch in the air. And the time to be gone has gone' (it would make a marvellous inscription above the booth for the Ghost Train). Harsent is much more a showman than a confessionalist; he whips out his box of horrors because he knows perfectly well it's what the audience craves. My only real answer is to invoke his predecessors: Thomas Lovell Beddoes, Christina Rossetti, Walter de la Mare. To give up on Harsent because he seems to delight in violent sensuality is to give up on *Goblin Market*. To give up on Harsent because the landscape he describes is perpetually tuned to dusk, and its inhabitants are perpetually going to the bad, is to give up on *The Listeners and Other Poems*. To give up on Harsent because, taken as a whole, his work is a wildly unrealistic carnival of blood and bones and things that go bump in the night, is to give up on *Death's Jest-Book*, not to mention *Titus Andronicus*.

One thing these predecessors have in common: they're all joyful, and are at their most joyful when cause for joy seems least inherent in their subject matter. Rossetti delighted more in describing goblin fruit and clawing fingernails than she ever did in affirming her belief in everlasting life. Walter de la Mare, when his emotions are sane and sensible ones, is second-rate even among the

Georgians; he comes good only when he's enjoying, say, the sight of rats in the ribcage of a corpse in a cellar. Beddoes, after one of the unluckiest lives on record, left perhaps the most heartbreaking suicide note in the world; his poetry, though ('Dream Pedlary' aside), possesses barely a trace of nineteenth-century melancholy; what replaces it is a very un-nineteenth-century exuberance.

One other thing I believe fervently about all three of these writers is that they would have enjoyed *Midsomer Murders*. The six episodes of this program which Harsent wrote don't fall into the category of work to be celebrated by this festschrift (they were done strictly for the money); I don't want to dwell on them or make them too central. Still, I find a continuity there: obviously the energies and preoccupations which find full release in Harsent's poetry are channelled only crudely into *Midsomer Murders*, but they are, nonetheless, recognisably the same energies. 'Cosy crime' was, I'm sure, intended as a derogatory name by whoever came up with it. In fact it's perhaps the animating paradox of the Romantics – given a certain background level of security, all crime is cosy, all bleak landscapes are beautiful, all horrors are familiar.

Anyway, I was pleased to find in Harsent's latest collection a poem which seemed to draw its inspiration almost explicitly from mystery drama:

> The hallway was empty, was endless. There were doors
> on either side. You can imagine it, can't you? The bare
> boards, the dado rail, a glint off the brass doorknobs,
> the way it fell away to fog and blur, the scent of almonds.

> (*Salt*, p. 58)

The 'scent of almonds', of course, was Agatha Christie's favourite piece of forensics; but 'the way it fell away to fog and blur' is a lively small-screen effect as well (in the opening credits of both *Poirot* and *Midsomer Murders*, the title swims up through the fog). And the glint off the doorknobs visible through the blur, as the camera gives us the perspective of the murder victim; the familiar swimming hallway. You can imagine it, can't you? If you can't, you can get plenty of practice by switching to ITV at 9pm on a weeknight.

These seem to me the essential things to say about Harsent: that he is primarily an optimist, a showman, and a Romantic, and criticism which misses these threads is liable to go badly wrong. There's also a real ground of kindness in his work, the white background on which his dark figures are most visible. (Harsent in a recent interview: 'Recently, I've been dreaming white landscapes, sometimes as observer, sometimes as fugitive.') This white background has become increasingly bright in the recent books. *Salt* includes some startling moments of tenderness:

> They could eat whenever they chose, they could go
> from place to place without having to say why, or sit
> in total darkness close enough to touch but never touching.

> (*Salt*, p. 87)

'They could eat whenever they chose' is superb: childlike, without feeling childish. The security, and the kindness which rises from security, are deftly handled. He can manage his grisly stage properties as well as ever: 'lees and leavings, slops, bone-ash, dieback and dreck; / hemp; her blood; the ejaculate of the damned' (p. 65). But underneath all this, he's a poet of genuine moral good sense, which is as much as to say that he's happy.

JOHN BURNSIDE

A poem for David Harsent,
in which the hare is only three parts metaphor

Unleashed, they are as quick
as whippets, cursed or blessed
with one man's hunger, scribbled out as whelps
of gunsmoke
in each cubicle of grass,

and yet the hare continues,
cast in bronze
and playful as we'd wish amidst the fake
Brancusis in this corporate hotel
garden, years

of meadowland, transistorised and lush
in rows of lavender, or marguerite,
a carry-home,
in cedarwood and tin,
to monetise *Arcadia* as *Ego.*

The new dogs spill from the Jeep.
They do not belong.
But, scrambling back and forth, in rutted loam,
they are starting to find the bones of a possible world,
caesuras of musk, the glit of a recent kill.

There is no guarantee they will live
through the next hard rain,
hunter and hunted drowned beneath careless stars
in miles of Yorkshire Fog
and shattered glass,

and yet the hare persists, beneath the moon,
for now, at least, the dogs gone home to dream
of all they love
and cannot run to ground,
the scentless night, the stars, the heart's safe-keeping.

FRED TAYLOR

Chalk and Clay:
David Harsent in Buckinghamshire

I first met David Harsent in the mid-sixties, in Aylesbury, which
is my hometown. The place was beginning to undergo drastic
changes. Nevertheless, it remained, for the moment, a fairly modest
market town, connected to but quite distinct from London. The
latter lay a little more than thirty-five miles to the south, accessible
either by Green Line Bus or rail (direct to Marylebone or change
at Amersham for the Metropolitan Line). Then again, you could
hitchhike it fairly easily, as I often did in my teens. Hardly anyone
we knew had a car.

The thing was, in 1952, Aylesbury had been declared an
'overspill' town, destined to accommodate surplus Londoners.
Slowly at first, but inexorably, the population began to increase,
from around twenty thousand at mid-century to thirty thousand
some fifteen years later (the town now has seventy-five thousand
inhabitants and is locked into a kamikaze course for a hundred
thousand by the 2020s).

There was something symbolic about the fact that in the fifties
and sixties Aylesbury – a Mercian town in Anglo-Saxon times –
became decisively disconnected from the South Midlands. The last
railway line leading northwards, to Rugby, was closed in 1966 as
part of the Beeching cuts to the railway system – I caught one
of the last trains to Manchester for an admission interview at the
university. Now we found ourselves drawn ever more strongly
southwards through the Chiltern Gap towards London. All rail
routes led to 'Metroland'. You could say that after 1966 we swung
away from the loam-rich but unsettling rural demi-paradise of
John Clare in the direction of the safe, semi-detached, mowed-
lawn kingdom of Betjeman.

Likewise, the lively but lazy-mouthed Estuarine accents of the new arrivals from London, matching their sassy big-city habits, had already begun to dominate the town's conversations. The new language vanquished the old as matter-of-factly and pitilessly as the grey squirrel drives out the red. The ancient and distinctive Bucks dialect was soon heard only from the elderly, or from the farmers and drovers who came in on cattle-market days, Wednesday and Saturday. When the market closed in the mid-1980s and was turned into a car park, Aylesbury lost a final link with its rural past. But then, by that time, almost the whole heart had been torn out of the town; the County Architect, Goering to his planning department's Luftwaffe, had made sure of it. A concrete Kasbah had replaced the cobbled lanes and pleasingly creepy shops around Silver (formerly Butcher) Street, the slaughterhouse and the shambles and the old market square. The underground section of the new shopping centre was used to shoot scenes for Stanley Kubrick's *A Clockwork Orange*.

I was born and mostly bred in Bucks, through my paternal grandparents. My mother was from the south coast, but had left London during the Blitz and found refuge among my father's relatives on the Buckinghamshire–Oxfordshire border. We simply stayed in Bucks after my father came back from war service in the Middle East.

David, of course, was born in Devon in December 1942. His father, who came from there, had already gone off to the war. The infant David soon found himself in Buckinghamshire because his mother's mother operated the switchboard at Princes Risborough post office, and accommodation in the form of a flat – plus child-care – was available 'over the shop'. The move to a council house came, as I recall, only after his father (whom little David had never previously laid eyes on) was demobbed in 1947.

David and I were both council-estate boys. If you are beginning to wonder, that being so, how and from where his preoccupations with nature came to him, perhaps it was that both our estates lay in those post-war days on the edge of town. Just a short skip (or sprint) of an after-school evening or weekend day and we were among fields, hedgerows and streams, animals and birds – not forgetting raptors and prey. In David's case, growing up in Princes Risborough, at the foot of the Chiltern Hills, midway between Aylesbury and High Wycombe, his territory was rising chalk upland, with birds wheeling overhead. Mine, on a development some way off the Oxford Road outside Aylesbury, began in the 1920s on what used to be a pig farm, was flat clay, intersected by ditches and liable to flooding. Birds tended to flock there at ground level.

David's boyhood in Risborough was different in another way. As a bright kid, he should have been directed towards the Royal Grammar School in High Wycombe, an altogether more prestigious place than my own mediocre Grammar in Aylesbury. I think there was talk of that, but as chance would have it (and a few other things that David could better explain than I) he was incapacitated when he should have been sitting the eleven-plus. In what one can only call a tragic and bizarre misallocation of resources, he was sent to the Technical School in Aylesbury.

Family circumstances meant that David had to end his formal education at sixteen with only two O-levels (English Language and English Literature) to his name, plus a certificate in metalwork. My parents had no money but the shelves in our house had books on them as well as souvenirs from seaside resorts, and they were ambitious for me and my siblings. In David's case, his parents (or at least – crucially – his father) were not. As for me, I ended up with something that David would and should have had, if he had wanted it: a scholarship to one of the ancient universities. Not that it stopped him, of course. Rather the opposite. His educational hunger remained gargantuan. But from an early age its assuagement was no longer a formal process.

There are almost exactly five years between us. David is actually just three months older than my big brother, Tom. I think they got to know each other as members of CND in the early sixties.

Anyway, it was through Tom, in around 1964, when I had just started in the sixth form, that we met. On leaving the Tech, David had told the Labour Exchange he liked books. This admission meant that in the Aylesbury of the time he was seen as having two obvious choices: he could become a proofreader at Hazell Watson & Viney, the large printing works on the Tring Road, which at one time employed a quarter of the town's entire working population; or he could get a job in a bookshop.

He chose (if that is the word) bookselling, and had been working in a bookshop – Weatherhead's, New and Antiquarian, in the centre of town – for some years when I met him. The atmosphere at the workplace was feudal. Benign – Frank Weatherhead was a decent man – but nevertheless decidedly feudal. David married young and by the age of twenty had a daughter. He, his then wife, Rosemary, and little Ysanne lived in tied accommodation owned by his employer in the village of Aston Clinton, on the Tring Road a five-mile bus ride from Aylesbury. This two-up-two-down labourer's cottage sat huddled within a terrace down a muddy lane. It was cold in the winter and damp all year round. Another child, a boy named Simon, arrived before long.

David, then as now almost preternaturally prolific, managed despite it all to get the necessary literary work done. He had been writing and submitting since his teens. However, it was at the cottage in Brook Street that he wrote poems that began to be published in magazines and in the *Times Literary Supplement*, where his work had caught the eye of Ian Hamilton. His extraordinary first collection, *A Violent Country*, was published by Oxford University Press in 1967, pretty much at the time I was matriculating at the university round the corner.

In its earliest stages, I think our friendship was an expression of mutual gratitude at finding someone else in Aylesbury who had read fairly widely and seriously and liked to talk about it – and, of course, make half-decent jokes, because serious can also be funny. There was a meagre selection of bohemian types in town, mostly hanging out in the Regent Coffee Bar or the Dark Lantern pub, but few seemed to have much ambition, intellectually or artistically. There was a lot of posing – *mehr Schein als Sein*, as the German phrase goes. And if you weren't a folk-music fanatic, finding further artistic stimulation within a thirty-mile radius presented a serious challenge.

Aylesbury to Oxford was about twenty-five miles, an hour and a half on a stop-everywhere bus that chugged back and forth several times a day. I was the only undergraduate I knew who did not arrive for the new term by train or car, but began each academic session by staggering, luggage and all, off the back platform of a decrepit double-decker at Gloucester Green bus station. *Brideshead Revisited* my time at the university was not.

David and I saw each other in the university vacations, mostly at his family home in Aston Clinton, talking ideas and politics and books, evenings fuelled by quarts of watery bitter fetched from the local pub, The Oak. I had realised pretty quickly that writing poetry was not my gift (David let me down gently), but that I was pretty adept at historical narrative and analysis (roughly in that order). I had also opted for a joint degree in Modern History and German, which was taking me in a firmly European direction. No problem. This gave us even more to talk about.

By the end of the 1960s, I was nervously motoring towards finals, while David had clearly begun to chafe at the limits of small-town life and the relentless routine of retail work. And by God, that cottage was damp. Then, in 1967, he won an Eric Gregory Award. It amounted to a lump sum that in retrospect was almost laughably small even by the standards of the time, but was more than he (or I) had ever laid hands on before. For David, it offered hope of a spell of uninterrupted writing, and perhaps even of an existential step-change. He took a chance and gave in his notice at Weatherhead's bookshop.

After finals, unsure of what would happen next, I went home to Aylesbury. David did get a lot of writing done. We also spent quite a lot of time trying our hands (unsuccessfully but entertainingly) at coarse fishing in the Grand Union Canal, which ran through the countryside not far from the cottage.

My joint degree results turned out lopsided: a first in history and a third in German. I did not get the year abroad that went with a pure Modern Languages course, and it showed. This was an uncertain summer for both of us. But in the end I scraped into a postgraduate place at Sussex to start research in German history.

David, with the grant money running out and in certain knowledge that at some point the tied cottage would have to be vacated, got another job. The daily commute south through Metroland it inevitably had to be – he would be writing copy for Associated Book Publishers in an office in Fetter Lane, on the edge of the City.

My own journeys soon took me altogether further east. I won a Volkswagen Research Studentship. While David rapidly built a successful publishing career and a brilliant writing reputation, I spent the next few years roaming around Cold War Germany, East and West, with an Olivetti portable and a few changes of clothes. It was the starting point of a creative arc that would prove less steep than my old friend's but which I am still quietly, though I hope with true Mercian grit, tracing today.

And we still talk about it all when we have the chance to be together.

RUTH PADEL

The Chimborazo Hillstar

For a week I saw no sky. The full moon
was a permanent fixture
above a city black as crêpe
where I lost myself in the swirl
of a one-way system

but each new morning she was still alive
I made it to the hospital car park

   I seemed to have paid a season ticket
   on my phone
   in a manner I do not remember

as night-workers were leaving
cleaners arriving by bus

I entered the dark maze of corridors
and followed blue floor arrows
the only route I knew   to where she lay.

Sometimes her eyes were closed.
Sometimes   I found her forcing herself to sip
a beaker of tea. She hated tea
but the coffee was worse.

We were on a planet of glass
about to shatter but we laughed
I read her *Emma*

she told the Bulgarian nurse
who kept urging her   pointlessly   to eat
that she preferred reality to fantasy
and talked of how she'd loved the Zoo.

The science   and romance
of a wilderness within the city
exquisite   endangered animals and plants

like *vulpes zerda*   little bat-eared Fennec
fox of the *Moonlight World*
staking his territory
across a miniature
Sahara of white sand.

She knew she was dying. *I'm on the way out*
was her mantra
         to nephews   nieces   friends
her last remaining brother.

The caves and valleys of her defences seemed to change
like the shifting floral fractures
flaws and gardens of the emerald
that give a stone its character.

Her determination   faced
with a moonlight world

of emboli and bedpans
     the morphine patch she insisted didn't work
         the aneurism that might pop any moment
kept reminding me of Chimborazo Hillstar
the highest-breeding hummingbird

still hanging on – thanks to nectar
in the orange flowers
of the *Chuquiragua* bush – where it evolved

up to the snowline of the Eastern Cordillera
and in the ravines   even in the caves
of golden Cotopaxi   Ecuador.

DECLAN RYAN

Opening Doors in the Head

In 2012 I was in the relatively early stages of a PhD on Ian Hamilton, and my supervisor, Jo Shapcott, put me in touch with David so I could interview him about the days of the *Review* and *New Review*, and everything around Hamilton's stint as the capo of Soho. To say he was generous with his time, and his insights, would be to undersell that first meeting – an anecdote about Hamilton's 'tempestuous' dinner with John Berryman being a particular highlight – but our conversation wasn't only helpful for my academic pursuits. His incisive reading of Hamilton's poems, and the colour he provided on what Hamilton used to refer to as his 'so-called literary life', was extremely clarifying, but David also spoke more broadly on writing, and the life built around it, in a way that – to quote one of his own phrases back at him – opened doors in my head. I've always had to juggle trying to write with a job or, more usually, jobs, and David's stories about the ways he'd balanced a life of poems with the necessity of making a living were not only encouraging, but also acted as a sort of reframing – he talked of having to create the environment in which poems can occur, as much in reference to Hamilton's spare output and 'miraculous persuasion' as in the immediate present, and it's an idea which has stuck with me ever since and to which I have, not always successfully, aspired.

While Hamilton's little magazine virus has never quite 'raged untreated' in me, I have always had some editorial ambitions and in 2013 a friend and I put together an anthology of mostly unpublished poets we liked and wanted to see more widely in print. In a fit of pique, chutzpah, or outright cheek I mentioned to my co-editor that I could perhaps ask David if he might be willing to read at our launch. Not only was he kind enough to read on the night, in a cramped basement on what turned out to be the hottest night since the sun was born, he also listened attentively and encouraged and corresponded with a number of the other readers, albeit having induced several near-faintings by reading from his recently published *Night*. He didn't have to do any of that, but his being there felt like a legitimising of what we were trying to do, at a point where we most needed to feel like this wasn't some grand delusion, or hobby that had got out of hand, and that it wouldn't always be self-produced anthologies or sweltering basements.

The following year I was selected to be part of the Faber New Poets scheme, out of which I got a pamphlet and, more importantly, the opportunity to work with a mentor of my choosing for four sessions over the course of a year. Having internalised Hamilton perhaps too fully by this point I was barely producing a poem from one month to the next, regrettably, but David (of course) was patient and encouraging in equal measure. The few poems I did write got the full Harsent treatment, which I quickly discovered meant a scalpel-sharp editorial eye and the sort of subtle, non-invasive comments that you're still thinking about months later, and which don't ever refer to the particular poem under discussion alone. David's was the sort of editorial advice which becomes part of one's inner monologue each time you sit down and so the sessions we had together in that year – which through my lack of productivity lurched into almost two – continue to colour my writing now.

Aside from the actual mentoring meetings, David's work-rate and range in the time I've known him have been a lesson in itself. From his stunning Yannis Ritsos translations to plays, libretti and of course the new collections of his own poems, David has managed to create the environment in which all this work happens, and will continue to, as well as demonstrating the need to try on new styles, forms and even disciplines to find the best way to say what one wants to say, and to never make the easy assumption that just because it's worked before it will again. One of the first insights

David gave me into Hamilton was a lunch they'd had around the time of David's *News From The Front* (1993). Hamilton, never a mentor but always a more-than-interested reader of David's work, while praising the book, mentioned in an off-hand way that David could write like that, but had he thought of what he might do next? Perhaps he could think about lengthening his line? The result was *A Bird's Idea of Flight* (1998), and while the story illustrates the fine margins involved in revolutionising a style as supple and finely tuned as David's, it also speaks to the emphasis he's always placed on being in motion, rather than resting in a mode, however successful he might be at it. There's a sense of continuity between the author of *A Violent Country* and *Salt*, a certain compression, lyrical tightening and focus, but the road taken from debut to latest collection is a study in refinement, experiment and restless pursuit.

The only thing David seems entirely unwilling to shift is his support of Chelsea FC, a briefly successful sports club based near his home. A perennial point of contention which has meant that, as a Spurs fan, watching football with him has never really been an option (although he did once rather magnanimously send me a message praising Erik Lamela's rabona in the Europa League – even team loyalties can't blind an aesthete). There are other sports, of course, and perhaps the most unlikely but brilliant evening I've spent in David's company was at the O2 Arena, watching a heavyweight boxing match in the hospitality seats, courtesy of his benevolent bank manager. It's probably no surprise that the author of *Fire Songs* got fully immersed in that near-murderous spectacle, and by the end was practically throwing jabs himself. Tragedy, violence, revenge and a baying crowd – who knows, there might just be an opera in that . . .

I read the story of the Livonian werewolves in Carlo Ginzburg's *Night Battles* – a book David gave me. It struck me that the process of writing poetry – at least the kind that David writes and that I, as his student, aspire to – might have some parallels with the werewolves' transformation and their subsequent bloody dash into hell.

Thiess of Kaltenbrun was put on trial for heresy in Jürgensburg, Swedish Livonia, in 1692. In his eighties then, Thiess admitted to being a werewolf and claimed he went to hell to fight with witches and the devil. Despite his testimony to the contrary, the judges believed he was turning people away from Christianity. He was sentenced to be flogged and banished for life.

The Livonian Werewolf

A student . . . came to a rabbi and said 'In the olden days there were men who saw the face of God. Why don't they anymore?' The rabbi replied, 'Because nowadays no one can stoop that low.'

(*Memories, Dreams, Reflections*, C. G. Jung)

Judge

. . . A 'wahrwolff' you say – was that something you willed?

Thiess

A madman in a sleazy bar made me a toast.
His hands trembled with soundless laughter
as he blessed me and spat. It spiralled from there.

The pelt was a gift: a farmer from Marienberg urged me
to take it; his prayer, a cry, I couldn't ignore,
though in truth, I cherished the skin for its warmth:

old blood on its muzzle, holes for ears.
Its dank, meaty smell was a comfort.
In the narrow strip at the season's cusp,

I strap it tightly to my body until my eyes lose white
and my teeth grow long. It's just as I say . . .
though, perhaps, on the Eve of St Lucie,

you'd have me lie down naked in a circle of trees, wait,
for the selfsame she-wolf of dreams to appear on soft feet
but that's all ash and air — what do I know of the workings of gift —

yet I ache for the change as I ache for a lover:
that blood-notes might pool in the hollow of my throat;
that my body brighten as the bony eye of the moon.

Judge

On the Eve of St Lucie, you and your pack travel to hell.
If 'Hounds of God' hate the devil so much, why do you go?

Thiess

Midsummer, midwinter and on the night of Pentecost,
we take our prey as wolves, eat it as men, roasted black over a fire
and always with salt, which the devil can't bear.

We know hell's breached by a narrow bridge suspended
over the swarming faces of the dead; faces
thrown up from the troubled core of nothing.

That ice on a bone-hungry wind is the least of it.
That earth's dead are silent but won't be still.
Beyond the abyss, gravel tracks lead straight

to the sunless swamp at Lemburg — just to look at the skim

is to sense yourself drowning: saltwater thick in your lungs,
the slow drift into darkness. Hell's cave is close by . . .

Judge

. . .And inside the cave?

Thiess

Fiends, demons, sorcerers, witches – Satan himself.
We break their limbs with iron bars, hack at their eyes,
then take up the wheat-germs and livestock stolen from the
   villagers –

whatever they've seized that might nourish the land.
Who else would risk the devil for the seed-grain of an unproved
   truth
and throw each blessing back to the wind?

Judge

The raw wound on your face – was that earned in a skirmish with Satan?

Thiess

I can't say for sure though dreamt I stood on a cliff-edge ready to
   leap
when a falcon stooped so close her wing-tip tore my skin.
Redemption's a hunter – lover or prey –

she delivers them both with feathers and blood.
I thought I could tame her – creance, a thread, tied to my wrist –
but each flight took the shape of unnameable risk.

This was my dream, though I've heard it said since,
a peasant called Skiestan struck my face
with a broom handle wrapped in a horse's tail.

Judge

The same peasant, Skiestan, who's been dead some thirty years?

Thiess

The dead remain vital in Satan's cause . . .

Judge

For the sake of your eternal soul, we urge you — repent.

Thiess

Repent, only to be locked away in the humdrum of the hour, numb
to the weight-in-stillness a moment before the season turns
and the old moon shifts in the palm of the sky?

You think I swear white is black and black, white,
for the sake of my eternal name?
That when I go seventy fathoms under the sea

to fight demons inside a fiery hell-hole for your sake,
I am of the devil's side?
No trace of the wolf in you, my lamb.

ANDRÉ NAFFIS-SAHELY

'You Thought Love Owed You Everything'

Originally published in *The Paris Review*

Opera can sometimes be a gory feast: Strauss's Salome kisses a severed head before being slain by Herod's soldiers, Britten's Peter Grimes drowns at sea after being chased by an angry mob, Tippett's King Priam is murdered after his entire family has either abandoned him or perished, while Puccini's Tosca leaps to her doom after her lover is shot by a firing squad. Yet all that violence is usually the bloody result of a genuine quest for love and liberty. Indeed, as Sir Harrison Birtwistle and David Harsent's latest chamber opera *The Cure* brilliantly shows, the moments we think will be our happiest can often turn into our most tragic. Jason and Medea have returned to Iolcos with the golden fleece so that Jason can finally reclaim his throne. However, Jason's father, Aeson, is on the verge of dying, and so Jason asks Medea the witch for yet another favour – as though killing her own brother to help Jason escape from Colchis hadn't been enough: 'I will give you children,' he says, 'Give Aeson back his youth'. Not because Jason loves his father, but because he wants the old man to celebrate his triumph and 'sing and dance with us'. It doesn't get more egotistical than that. Nobody asks the old king whether he wants to drink from the fountain of youth, they simply force it down his throat:

Aeson

(angry and perturbed)

What you've made of me is what I must become.
More chance of sadness; more chance of loss;
another trudge into old age, waiting
for my sight to fail, my hearing to fail, my body to weaken ...

Aeson (cont . . .)

I had lived my life. Now I have time back I am lost in time;
I must live my past again as another man.

I could smell death: something of richness in it
I could see death: vast and shadowless
I could hear death: voices drifting to silence.

My last thought before sleeping
My first thought on waking:
Death   death   death   death   death

Harsent has a knack for exploding human certainties, in this
instance the assumption that we'd all like to be young forever;
his Aeson actually understands that life is worth losing, but must
nonetheless endure his son and daughter-in-law as they keep
him alive purely to suit their own purposes. A supremely gifted
librettist, Harsent understands that 'the gods punish hubris' and
that 'everyone is guilty', but that the trick lies in picking a specific
moment and mood in a story to slide the spectator into the heart
of these dilemmas. It's the composer's duty to sustain that mood,
and there's a wonderful section ten minutes into the opera where
Medea calls out the names of the 'herbs that harm to cure':

Horehound sysmera   woundwort

sanicle   lupine saxifrage

Birtwistle's score, with its hypnotic, repetitious use of the E note,
perfectly frames the words with its bold, sharp contours, ensuring
the violin, viola and cello don't drown the voices. In the end,
Aeson's youth is restored, but he storms off after violently kissing
Medea, throwing her to the ground when he's done with her.
Hardly the reward Medea was expecting. Further complicating
matters, Aeson and Jason are now almost indistinguishable — a

visual element reinforced by the fact the tenor Mark Padmore plays both roles – shaking the foundation of Medea's love for Jason – hitherto blind and absolute – and signalling the birth of her new-found independence.

The *New York Times* has called the Harsent-Birtwistle team – whose collaboration began with *Gawain* (1991) and continued with *The Woman and the Hare* (1999), *The Ring Dance of the Nazarene* (2003), *The Minotaur* (2008), *The Corridor* (2009), *Songs from the Same Earth* (2012) and now *The Cure* – 'an alchemically potent pairing' and while Harsent has pointed out that 'opera is about the music, since few people speak of Da Ponte's *Don Giovanni* or Piave's *La Traviata*', I'd like to see anyone argue that Mozart's greatest operas – *The Marriage of Figaro*, *Don Giovanni* and *Così fan tutte* – weren't also achieved thanks to Lorenzo Da Ponte's vast talents. After all, Da Ponte was so sought-after most composers in Vienna fought over him.

Britain's greatest living poet, Harsent is nearing the end of what has been an amazingly fertile decade, which began with the Forward Prize-winning *Legion*, a sequence of poetic dispatches from various parts of our war-torn world, and concluded with *Fire Songs*, which was awarded the T. S. Eliot Prize, is dedicated to Birtwistle, and is a sequence of hallucinatory reflections on how our world might end: 'My children's children will stand outside the law, to wreck / and break, to witness, to set fires, to fall on the weak.'

Onto *The Corridor*, *The Cure*'s companion piece. The setting is the liminal moment in the Orpheus and Eurydice myth, when Orpheus turns to look at his beloved when she's just a couples of paces shy of returning to the world of the living. Premièred in 2009, this chamber opera was revived so it could be performed back to back with its younger sibling, with the outstanding Mark Padmore and Elizabeth Atherton playing both Jason-Aeson/ Medea and Orpheus/Eurydice. Needless to say, the Orpheus myth is one of the most patronising to women: it's all about *his* pain, *his* misfortune, *his* attempt to rescue her, *his* lyre, while Eurydice has instead usually stood around like a prop. No longer. Alison Chitty's set for *The Corridor* should be commended for visually balancing the story in Eurydice's favour, allowing her far more room to roam than her impatient lover: Orpheus stands on one side of a doorframe, atop a square of bright, almost uninviting green, with Eurydice on the other, surrounded (and dressed in) a soothing slate grey. The lighting also has the effect of making Orpheus's side of the world seem far more inhospitable than the world of the dead, making the green glow like ectoplasm rather than soft, welcoming grass.

The beginning is bold but simple, the quasi-monosyllabic dialogue punctuated by Birtwistle's staccato notes, especially around the word 'light' as the couple makes its way back to the world of the living. By the time Eurydice reaches the far end of the aisle, she staggers and an argument ensues. Birtwistle and Harsent once again trump convention and restore Eurydice's multidimensionality. She has a cutting rebuttal to every single answer Orpheus provides to her question:

> *woman*
> – you looked back because –
>
> *man*
> – because you seemed to be already there –
>
> *woman*
> – because the moment seemed more yours than mine –
>
> *man*
> – because I felt you step into the light –
>
> *woman*
> – because you felt I'd be there as I should –

man
– because love brought me round –

woman
– because you thought love owed you everything –

Like Aeson, Eurydice was never desperate to be rescued, or at least didn't think of it as such an uncomplicated proposition. She's no damsel in distress, and actually seems quite at home in the underworld. Harsent and Birtwistle make Eurydice the real star. Orpheus sings, but Eurydice makes *sense*. For instance, this following passage is in a kind of *sprechgesang*:

Suppose he'd brought me out; imagine that –
the blaze of noon, unbearable, the wind
sour in my nostrils, grass like flint underfoot,
his spittle stinging my lip,
a tangle of voices, urgent, meaningless,
my true language the soft
hints and gentle laughter of the dead.

In life he loved me; in death he loved me more –
my second life his gift to both of us;
my second death to be mine and mine alone.

What did he want from me? – My love his due,
my return to the world of light his masterstroke.

Eurydice also knows her lyre-wielding lover is doomed: 'his grief will become his token, his name / another word for loss: all he's remembered by', she says, knowing Orpheus is doomed to be ripped apart by the maenads, Dionysus's mad, lustful acolytes. We all know how the story ends: Orpheus loses his nerve an inch shy of victory, turns, and thus loses her forever. Here is the end of Orpheus's song:

There's only one word
dark enough, one word as bleak, as cruel,
as blighted, as unnatural, one word
to uproot the tongue, to deafen, to break bones,
to tear the heart, a word to blacken rain,
to rot fruit on the bough, to poison streams,
to still the child in the womb, to bring to ruin
all joy or gift or courage or hope or love —

SIMON HARSENT

On Collaboration

Being asked to write about my collaborations with my father is not only daunting, but also incredibly difficult. Firstly, because I have to write, which is not my skill; I'm a dyslexic son of a poet, and I think I was destined to be a visual artist. Secondly, it stirs up an awful lot of emotions, and that's not always easy terrain to navigate. My relationship with my father has always been a complex one, an intense one. It is, for the most part, loving and filled with admiration, but also – as I'm sure most children feel – full of a need for acceptance and approval.

I believe our collaborations started years ago – if not the collaborations themselves, then the seeds of them in our ability to do so.

When I was a child, I would sit in my father's study while he wrote. I sat in silence, looking at books of painters such as Rembrandt and Van Gogh. For me, it was time with my father – a chance for me to be in his company – but it was far more than that. It was in these moments that I gained an education that it's impossible to find elsewhere.

That experience shaped my life in so many ways. I was learning without even realising it. I was learning about art by studying these books but, more importantly, I was learning about sensibility. I learnt how to be emotionally moved by art when I was in that room, losing myself in paintings that were truly transformative and which transported me elsewhere. To this day, I am comfortable sitting silently in a room with someone I love, both of us immersed in something.

So much of what I have done since, and still do now, has been driven by my times with my father and his encouragement for what I do. Time spent at galleries with him, looking and talking about the works, informed a very impressionable young man that life is not lived on the surface – it is lived in the depths and in the shadows. It's what the artist brings to the creative process that informs the final piece. The first decision he or she makes while exploring a subject determines the next decision and so on, leading them on a uniquely personal journey which defines both artist and art. This process is not a technical exercise; art is reaction and emotion informed by our past experiences.

A lot of my work is concerned with how one's choices define one's future, and how we are destined to become a product of our environment, which is, in turn, defined by those choices.

So, as I say, the collaborative process started many years ago.

When we work together, it just seems to happen. It's never explicitly talked about, never planned, but just happens. We've never had to go looking for something to work on together; opportunities simply present themselves. Obviously, it was something I had always dearly wanted to happen, but I suspect that trying to force a project would have ended up with something contrived and less successful.

Our first collaboration was *Into the Abyss*. I had just finished shooting a series of images of a woman underwater, struggling to resurface. As with all my work, it was partly biographical. I knew I had something, but I felt the images were so different from other projects I had been working on, they needed to exist somewhere else in some other form. I sent them to David and asked him whether he saw anything in them that might spark something.

For both of us it seems to make most sense when David's work responds to mine. I think it would be a very different prospect the other way around, and I'm not sure whether it would be as successful.

Collaborating with my father feels like being that boy in the room, again, all those years ago. It's an easy, natural process, being together. We share the same experience, the same artistic space, but both of us are in our own thoughts.

SEAN O'BRIEN

Save the Last Dance for Me

for D.H.

Masquers, slowly dancing, torchlit, on the furthest quay.
Arlecchino, Colombina, Punchinello, Il Dottore.

The fever in the blood has thickened to an ooze
But still – see there – it burns, about the eyes and fingertips

And when the lady turns away and back and licks her lips.
The ultimate infirmity is needing not to choose.

★

There are sins of the flesh. There are lies of the mind.
Each betrayal is paid in kind.

Il Capitano, La Signora, Scaramouche.
First with the daughter, then with the wife,

With the blue-black kiss of a fisherman's knife.
Tincture of mercury. Scald and douche.

Time they were gone. Too soon for dawn.
Gates of ivory? Gates of horn.

★

Unlisted it would seem in *la Commedia del' Arte*,
You, sir, what do you bring to the party?

Crossing the marsh in your weightless craft,
With a gaze that glitters like burning gold,

In a hand as ancient as the oar you hold
You have already finished the final draft.

PATRICK DAVIDSON ROBERTS

The Biographer's Misgivings
& three sketches

All roads do not lead to David Harsent, but enough do. In 2014 I made the decision to write a book about him and set to knocking up one of those full author bibliographies that can act as a road map in such projects. The useful thing about decent poets is that these bibliographies tend to be small. Seven pages later I was having fourth and fifth thoughts. Television scripts, thrillers, libretti and lyrics. Introductions, translations. I hadn't even got onto the poetry, which was really why I was here.

I came to, and remain at, the conclusion that David is a form of *sampo*, that odd fire-forged device of the Finnish national story, the Kalevala. Forged in the dark woods of that land, after much mad and magic struggle, the *sampo* is a metal machine that provides salt, wheat and gold in limitless supply to whomever owns it. The essentials, sure, but its appearance is far too early in the tale for that to be a good thing, a thing *settled* on. There is much of David in that.

There are two meetings that you have with poets – on the page and in person. One of the few things that John Clegg and I agree on is the brilliance of David's *Legion*, and that was my first meeting, at twenty, in a new city, with a new poet. I read 'Sniper' in a Foyles:

> I am tucked up here, a sure thing, with my sausage and beer
> and a field-stove to keep my fingers supple. Days pass.
> I'm more than content in my snuggery, my lair;
> I have somewhere to lay my head and somewhere to piss
> and, for comic disputation, the birds of the air.

> ('Sniper', *Legion*)

It would be years before I learnt about the role of Goran Simić and Sarajevo in David's warscapes, in *Legion* in particular, but as a child of the '90s, spending most nights watching the footage of Bosnia on *Newsround*, this was a language and transmitted imagery that I knew. As always with David there is that chill. No Ginsbergian 'I am with you' to the victim. For the first half-decade or so of reading David I read him with a clenched hand, waiting for the poem to lunge out of the page at me. I was wary. But I was still reading.

★

Summer, 2014. I've decided to start writing a book about him. He's doing a reading later that day at Regent's Park Zoo and wants to wander over there during the day to see where it's happening. We meet at Baker Street and head for the park to have something approaching a picnic there beforehand. We sit on the grass in the sun, him in sunglasses. As I start to lay out the general idea for the book that I want to write it becomes apparent that he cannot hear me properly. For once our shared oracular affliction — tinnitus — and my particular problem (mumbling) have aligned, and we are almost rendered incommunicable. Somehow we make it to the Zoo.

I mention this to him two years later; the inauspicious start to a project which relies on regular, distinct communication, begun in white noise and silence. 'Of course,' he replies, 'it's good to get down to first principles.'

★

Years after reading 'Sniper' in Foyles, when I eventually met David it was to ask about Ian Hamilton. I'd gone through *Another Round at the Pillars*, the festschrift that David had edited for Hamilton, and emailed or rung up most of the contributors. Generally speaking, the novelists of Hamilton's crowd spoke of his kindness but were loath to hand any kind of debt over to (of all things) a poet, in terms of their subsequent successes. The poets were a different story. They all gladly acknowledged Hamilton's role in their work, their lives, and any real success that it is possible for a poet to have. Almost the first thing that David said to me was 'Ian was the *coolest* person that I've ever known'. It's the only time that I've ever heard him use that word, and although it took a while to realise, there was something trusting in his using such a (for him) fulsome expression in a sentence, when in conversation with a stranger.

Is all of this sounding a bit luvvie, confirmation of the kind of insiderish thought that any mention of poetry in the wider world fixates on? Yes, it is. As his biographer I am caught in the grip of an unabashed admiration and coinciding defensiveness about David. He's both subject and friend. Impartiality never stood a chance. Simon Armitage has it right when writing about Ted Hughes: 'We had certain interests in common but our meetings were by definition lopsided because one of my interests was him.'

A paradox that, to my mind, only Hamilton and Andrew Motion have evaded when writing biographies about poets they had known is that their knowledge of and interest in the subject is serious and undeniable, but that both, almost by definition, render them to a certain extent untrustworthy. What chance of balance, of perspective, of context? Little. All I can hope to offer – at this stage, at least – is some exploration of source and subject – the places where I think the man and poems touch.

★

Winter, late 2016. After an afternoon of discussing Legion *and* Night *he suggests that we go to his local Indian restaurant. It's a quiet evening and there are three couples spread around the dark room. We make the fourth and sit in the window. At one point during conversation I allude to a recent unsuccessful encounter and reflect on the absence of an expected criteria for professing your bisexuality during a heterosexual date. He looks up.*

'I didn't know that you were bisexual"

I don't say anything. I am eating, after all.

He methodically looks at the three other couples, as if accrediting them. A waiter wanders towards us. Then, his cutlery re-engages and he says:

'Well. I'm not sleeping with you.'

The waiter swerves the table.

★

At the end of the Kalevala the *sampo* has been shattered into pieces that are then made into jewellery that the surviving characters swear will bring them luck, warm beds and full stomachs. It's long on record that David's primary interest in the short, stark poetry printed in Hamilton's *Review* was in trying to thread these lyric fragments into a narrative necklace, so perhaps the *sampo* analogy pays off. Things wrought from breakage and shatter into new sequence and production. To paraphrase Lawrence Durrell on Cavafy: it is here that most I find him.

I am yet to meet someone born during the Second World War who is entirely seamless, and David is no exception. Add to this the fall down the stairwell onto a concrete floor as a child, and the resultant long convalescence that led to his bedbound encounter with the border ballads. Add also the father returned from a long war. The idea of fracture becomes all too tempting to follow. However, to my mind it escapes the real fundamental of David. His eye, his pen, even his approach to a conversation is about *join*. I do not think that this is a reaction to the breakages – an attempt to fix things; rather, he sees the whole picture. The complete. There is no interest for him in fragments – that's the secret to his complexity, or one of the secrets.

You can tell a David episode of one of the series he worked on for television – not so much the procedurals such as *Midsomer Murders*, but the 'continuals': *The Bill*, or *Holby City* – fairly easily. His episodes, while they may make a passing gesture (often of the two-fingered kind) to the running themes or stories, are self-contained narratives and concerns. The episodes before or after a Harsent block may be of romance, intrigue or scandal with the regulars, but the episode beginning with hellfire, death, silence, or white noise is concerned with a story of its own. That these episodes of his making add to rather than detract from the program as a whole is a testament to the Jacobean nature of David's long-game.

Something similar can be said about his execution of the Stella Mooney detective series. It is a series, yet somehow the concerns are total within the space of the individual stories, and sometimes in the space of a single chapter. A chapter at the bar with Mooney is often enough to dwarf the case unfolding throughout the next hundred pages – eternity in an hour.

Intriguingly, for me, David's completeness has never been embodied by a specific form. While there is a Harsentian tone, a Harsentian idiolect, there has never been a dependable Harsentian poem. Like Larkin, he experiments with innovation ('Elsewhere' in *Night* and 'Sang the Rat' in *Fire Songs* being the most impressive examples of ambition matched with invention), but like that poet he also believes strongly in the enduring relevance of the recognisably poetic. Fiona Sampson rightly observed that David has not just the border ballads but also the Baptist hymnal as a touchstone, and this latter item is (ironically, for a denomination not known for its flexible outlook) almost defined by its metamorphic structure.

To my mind it's become an unhelpful aspect of David's critical reception that people divide his career into short-line and long-line stages. The former is thought to occupy the first five of his collections, and the latter the six that have come since. The poet himself has not been uninvolved in this myth-making, it must be said, and perhaps he and others are right. I am unconvinced, partly because poetry that's worth anything does not conform to such niceties, and also because it requires a demonstrable unfolding of language and tone that I think robs David's early work of the subtlety inherent therein.

It is true that as David's lines have grown (generally accepted as everything written from *A Bird's Idea of Flight* onwards) then the physical capacity for exposition and exploration has widened, too. You see this most clearly in a piece like the opener to *Fire Songs*:

Anne, you are nothing to me. Only that you knew best
how to unfasten your gown while they waited at the rack.

Only that *she was hard prest*
which I now can't shake from my mind.

[. . .]

       as she cracks and splits, as she renders to spoil:
the only thing she can get to me through the furnace, as I lean
in to her, is *yes, it will be fire it will be fire it will be fire* . . .

                                  ('Fire: *a song for Mistress Askew*')

I am two years into an argument with a fine poet whose genuine
discomfort with the level of detail shown here (and elsewhere)
precedes and dictates his admiration of lines like that last one.
Again, here, is the chill. That 'you are nothing to me' forces the
question: *then why describe her fate in such lurid detail?* The answer is
that to imply is not enough, is certainly not enough with someone
as used as Anne Askew was. The depiction must be complete, and
the completion is wound into a distinctly prickly piece of verse
with that repetition.

    This completeness, and the prickle, has long been there in David's
work; however, as the following from *Mister Punch* demonstrates:

    In stark sorrow he straddled his hand,
    torso dim in the full-length glass,
    the yellow night-light
    staining his arm and naked haunch.

    From knees to neck
    a bundle of stumpy joints like truncheons;
    an amputee
    wizened by week-long fasts in the littered room.

                             ('Schiele: Standing Self-Portrait')

If you consider (and I do) syllabics and metre to be part of the same machinery as phonetics and lexis itself, then the prickly repetition is here too ('*torso dim* in the *full*-length *glass*'), just as the completeness is, in the space described ('full-length').

David's form shifts because different poems have to do different things. But the concern has always been that of the complete, of the full – after all, even the *sampo* didn't just provide one thing.

★

March 2017. This time we've decided that the pub will finish the interview. We're about to leave the house. On the request of the occupant of the living room, he firmly tugs the door to that room shut. The handle (of course) comes off in his hand, the door hits the frame and begins to re-enter the room, much to the displeasure of its occupant. For the first time, I see him completely bewildered, as he dives first for the inaccessible top of the door, then the sides, and finally the base as we attempt to close the thing. By the time we're out of the house the certainty is back, and the door handle in his jacket pocket.

★

As far as I've been able to draw a conclusion, it is this. As a poet, David's achievement is one of constant renewal, informed by the interplay between a need to depict the full, the complete, and the constantly shifting transmission and form of that depiction. Things change, permanently, in a bacterial metamorphosis, from those threaded-together *Review*-era poems through to last year's *Salt*. He is more certain than anyone else I've encountered of the need to say everything, certain that the telling should not stop. For my money he is our best poet since Larkin (where else do you get to say these things), and I look forward to the next ten pages of the bibliography.

HUGO WILLIAMS

Back to Princes Risborough

Originally published in 'Freelance',
Times Literary Supplement, in October 2007

The poetic careers of David Harsent and myself have run parallel ever since we first met, under the Ian Hamilton umbrella, in the mid-1960s. We both had *Review* pamphlets published in 1969 and we both appeared as 'Hugo Harsfried' in one of Clive James's long poems in 1974. Born, like me, in 1942, David was brought up in the Buckinghamshire town of Princes Risborough, while I lived a mile away in the village of Whiteleaf. He lived in a flat above the Post Office, while I resided in the sturdy Whiteleaf House. My father's fortunes took a turn for the worse in 1949 and we moved to a flat in Brighton, but Whiteleaf was where the magic started and where it has remained: something about an avenue of trees that led up to a white cross cut in the hillside, clearly visible from Risborough.

The other day, David told me he was going back to look at his old flat and wondered if I'd like to go along. He particularly wanted to see the thirty-foot stairwell he'd fallen down, aged eleven, a fall which cost him his eleven-plus. I can see that this might not be everyone's idea of a fun outing, but David is aware of my backward-facing enthusiasms.

The first surprise is that everything is exactly as he described it, only more so. Here is the red brick Post Office, now a sorting office. Here is the yard where the coke pile stood, a mountain then. Over there is the dispatch platform that doubled as a cowboy camp. Here is the bike shed, still housing a single mouldy delivery bike, where the ten-year-old poet kissed his cousin. David stands in the yard and stares, seeing things I can't see, but can almost see, having played the same games myself at the same time. He points to the window of the flat from where his mother saw his father getting off the bus after the war. He swivels his arm. 'At that bus stop over there.' She hadn't seen him for four years and promptly fainted with delayed relief. Nearby is the British Legion, which his father, a council bricklayer, helped to build every Saturday. Opposite the Post Office is Carlton House, once the Carlton Cinema. Over there is his school, the Princes Risborough County Primary School, changed, suitably, to an old people's home. It strikes me that there is an Englishness to this suburban scene that has mostly disappeared from today's countryside, a glimmer of hope that some things can be trusted to sit still, if only from dumb stupidity.

We have arranged to meet up with Post-Master Jasjit Dhillon, who has agreed to unlock the past for us and show us around. We begin at the side door. 'Is this the same bell?' I ask. 'Yes, but the door was always open.' Jasjit leads the way down to the cellar, where we stand watching David regress to a little boy, contemplating his erstwhile dungeon. 'This is where Mr Bernard the boiler-man sat in his rocking chair with a rug thrown over it, eating apples with a knife.' I imagine him rocking away in his cosy hideout, staying warm in the bitter days of 1947.

Now here is the brutal concrete stairwell we have come to see. The single luxury of the hallway is the original polished banister, the cause of David's downfall. 'I used to lean over, not straddle it, and one day I leant over too far. I remember seeing a crack in the ceiling as I went down and thinking that I must tell my father about it.' He was badly concussed and unable to take his eleven-plus. He passed the thirteen-plus and should have gone to High Wycombe Grammar School, but his father didn't want him travelling so far, and he had to go to Risborough Technical College. 'I'm quite pleased to have my Ordinary National Certificate in Metalwork', David says.

The top floor of the Post Office has been stripped and vandalised, but David is transfixed. To the left of the stairs was the telephone exchange, where his granny was the night telephonist. 'This little room was where she slept when she was on duty. Almost no one rang up in the night then, but if they did, my granny had to get up, put on her wraparound bakelight headset and say "Hello caller, what number do you require? Put four pennies in the box please.'"The Harsents had no telephone themselves, but his mother was one of the daylight operators: my parents must often have spoken to her.

On the right of the stairs is a tall room without any windows and, beyond that, the door to the family flat, inhabited by four generations of women, until his father came home. Gingerly we step over the threshold into 1940s Britain. By virtue of its ruined condition, almost like a skilfully dressed film set — high ceilings, high cream gloss, the parquet floor pulled up he used to slide on — the flat seems timeless, as if the family have just moved out. 'This was grandma's room,' David tells us. 'Holman Hunt's *The Light of the World* used to hang over there and the light would travel round her room.' In here was where his great-grandmother slept: 'Whisky before meals, brandy for digestion.' And here was the tap in the kitchen under which his father would hold his head to cool the piece of shrapnel lodged there. 'All of this is totally unchanged,' he repeats, as he touches a surviving doorknob and performs the compulsive repetitive routine he used to put himself through as a child. He shows us the high cupboard hanging open in the hall where his grandfather's mysterious hoard of inflationary deutschmarks was stashed — the nearest he ever came to an inheritance. By the time anyone realised that they were valuable as Nazi relics, his grandfather was dead and the cash had been burnt in Mr Barnard's boiler.

The 1940s tiled fireplace has somehow survived in the onetime living room, and we clearly see David's father, always known as 'Snips', from 'Harsnips', kneeling on the bare boards lighting the fire. 'My mother would be laying the table for tea. The tablecloth would billow up . . .' There is an old table in the room and I see the cloud of linen hovering over it. One Christmas day they sang 'Daisy, Daisy' to their son, before taking him into the hall where a new bike was standing. The story replicates exactly my memory of my own first bike, waiting for me in the hall at Whiteleaf, a mile away, on that same Christmas Day in 1948.

A few days after our visit, David called up his Aunt Elaine, now seventy-three, and happened to mention the tall windowless room at the top of the stair. That was the strong room, she told him. The original door was made of steel. One day during the war, a number of security guards came to the Post Office and the nine-year-old Elaine was told that something was going on which she should keep to herself. The guards positioned themselves on every second step and started passing hundreds of gold bars up the stairs and into the tall room, where they were stacked on reinforced shelves. The room was then sealed for the duration of the war.

RICHARD SCOTT

4th Innocent

4th Innocent:
(Distant)
Olola . . .

The countertenor's voice, the male alto, has long been associated with human sacrifice. In Britten's second *Canticle* a countertenor sings the role of Isaac, the boy his father Abraham would stab and bleed. In Handel's *Theodora* a counter tenor sings the role of Didymus the Roman soldier who is beheaded and burnt. And in Harrison Birtwistle and David Harsent's opera *The Minotaur*, two countertenors play the 4th and 5th Innocents who are gored and eaten by the half-man, half-bull monster. Maybe this is because the countertenor sings high. Maybe this is because his singing voice is plaintive, perhaps like a scream. Or maybe this is because the origins of his voice lie in castration. The Baroque male altos had their genitals removed to ensure their boyish treble voices would last into puberty and adulthood. Sometimes this was performed in a milk bath. The boy was fed opium and his carotid artery compressed. Backstreet surgeries in Naples and Rome where these castrations were carried out bore the sign HERE BOYS ARE CASTRATED. The wellbeing of these beautifully talented boys was sacrificed to something bigger. In the Baroque Era there was something bigger than individual wellbeing. Maybe this was music. Maybe this was God. Gods have always demanded blood; it's been used the world over for every kind of ritual and spell. Blood is potent. The most potent ingredient.

O: That I was very much a sacrifice. There was a strong sense of utter vulnerability about us. The total inevitability of our deaths. R: Do you remember the text at all? I remember these vowels. O: I seem to remember it was an ancient language. Was it Greek?! R: Maybe chopped-up Greek? Like *Io Moi*. O: Yes! That rings a bell. R: Also *O-lo-lo-lo, O-lo-lo-lo-lo-la!* O: The whole thing made me feel like a sacrifice. R: Yes? Why? O: We seemed incidental, disposable, and yet essential. R: If we didn't die then Theseus couldn't have come to kill the Minotaur. Dan doesn't know what *Io Moi* means btw. He says *Gie Mou* means my son. Maybe that's it? O: Was there something about us being extra vulnerable because our words were maybe untranslatable? R: You remember the conductor who just kept saying sing anything you like but sing it in rhythm. O: LOL. Something like, scream all you want . . .

Ovid writes of a white bull walking out of the sea, beautiful and shining, which King Minos of Crete was supposed to sacrifice but couldn't. And this refusal led to so much bloodshed and enforced sacrifice. His wife Pasiphaë, meaning 'all light', was cursed with lust for and then raped by the bull. Ten months later she gave birth to a hybrid creature; *twin form of bull and man*. And King Aegeus of Athens, because Minos' son had been murdered on Athenian soil, sent seven boys and seven girls to Crete every year to maintain an uneasy truce between the two kingdoms. And these fourteen nameless boys and girls on the cusp of puberty were sacrifices. They were fed to the Minotaur. No one really knows what he, the Minotaur, did to them. Probably he ate them. Maybe he tortured them before he ate them as predators sometimes do. Ovid writes that he was *nourished on blood* so maybe he drank their blood. Once they arrived on the beach at Crete, these stolen children, they were forced, one by one, down into the labyrinth. The labyrinth that was built by the craftsman and mystic Daedalus to house a monster and a blood ritual. The labyrinth which had as many pathways as flowing water. The labyrinth in which Minos believed he could hide shame itself.

4th Innocent:
(Closer still)
Io moi moi

In 2008 and again in 2013 I sang the role of 4th Innocent in Harrison Birtwistle and David Harsent's opera *The Minotaur.* And because you can't have a labyrinth on stage — the audience wouldn't be able to see what lay behind the maze'd walls — the labyrinth, with all its blood-splashed corridors, was a video. A red cursor slipping along black, angular and pre-programmed passageways. There was also a video of the sea, because we crossed the sea to get there. The sun and moon were spotlights. The rags we wore were organic, made-to-measure cotton smocks. You don't bleed on stage. Stage blood is a mixture of chocolate syrup and red food colouring and is poured into these tiny water balloons. You don't die on stage either. When we were gored we had to drag a blood sack along our flank or neck, exerting just enough pressure for it to pop and gush like arterial spray. The Minotaur didn't gore us, he didn't chase us; our death scenes were slowly and patiently choreographed over twelve weeks in a mirror-lined ballet studio with sprung wooden floors. The Minotaur was also an opera singer. His horns and muzzle were fashioned from chicken wire. Nothing on stage is real.

4th Innocent:
(Closer still)
Olola ...
Olola
... Olola ...

4th Innocent was not the first sacrificial victim I had played on stage. When I was eleven I took the role of Iphigenia in my school play, and four nights in a row Jonathon, my friend from swimming class, stabbed and bled me with a wooden dagger. He needed a good wind to sail to Troy. I wore my mum's Manhattan Rose lipstick. I also wore her clip-on brass earrings but they were too heavy and kept tugging at my lobes so I took them off after the first night. To prepare for the sacrifice our drama teacher made everyone watch *A Short Film About Killing*. My dad found it in the international section at Blockbuster Video. The next day the entire cast burst into the dining hall during lunch break, grabbed me and carried me aloft to the rehearsal room, all the while shouting KILLKILLKILL. The dinner ladies didn't know what was happening so one called the police. Another pulled the fire alarm.

There is an opera by Gluck in which Iphigenia narrowly escapes being murdered by her own father. At the last moment, just before the dagger pierces her jugular, she is spirited away by a goddess and lives out her days as a priestess on this remote Greek island. Ironically, though, the religion she is in service to demands that she sacrifice all and any strangers the moment they set foot on her remote shores. And this Old World call for blood is further complicated by the arrival of her shipwrecked brother Orestes and his boyfriend Pylades. But somehow, after four very involved and lengthy acts, the boys' lives are spared. *Iphigénie en Tauride* is an unusually clement opera. Maybe it is their beautiful singing; both individually in tortured and coloratura-filled arias, and together in a lilting and lamenting duet sung in the bowels of the temple's dungeon. Or maybe it is because neither of them is a countertenor; they sing in their baritone and tenor, or broken voices. Or maybe it is because Orestes is not exactly innocent; he has, after all, just murdered his mother Clytemnestra. It is usually innocence that is sacrificed in opera. The death of the innocent is the engine of operatic drama.

4th Innocent: For a libretto written by a poet, many of the characters
in *The Minotaur* are surprisingly wordless. The Minotaur

himself only speaks in dreams, otherwise he bellows. *(Un-
intelligible).* And the Innocents, mostly we sang what I first
took to be vowels or plaintive vocalises. *Io moi moi. (BTW,
Dan now thinks that maybe it might mean* O my Goddess*).*
And Ariadne, the prima donna, who paced the shores of
Crete waiting for the boatload of us quivering sacrificial victims; Ariadne who saw the black-sailed boat approaching at dawn; Ariadne who led us all into the black
labyrinth; well, she got all the best lines to sing. I was so
jealous of her.

'the black muzzle wet from the caul,
the black pelt, the black and bony brow, the horn-buds,
    the fat tongue
that slapped out at the birth-blood . . .
This creature, this half-and-half, this hair-and-horn
humpback, hideous, this child of the bull from the sea . . .'

Ariadne sang all the gorgeous alliteration. She sang all the
insistent repetition that became like a chant, like a prayer.
She sang all the gently seesawing phrases, for the Minotaur was never just one thing, he was always half-this and
half-that. Everything that came out of her mouth was so
fabulously bloodied, so Old World, so ancient.

4th Innocent:
...who likes not cattle-cake, but bone...

I had one intelligible line. *Who likes not cattle-cake, but bone*. I was so proud of that line. I remember spitting out the double C's with such tortured joy. And Birtwistle set the word *bone* to this descending, atonal arpeggio that I had to chest, darken with my broken voice, so I channelled my inner prima donna and chested like Bartoli. I made those seven words so drama. That single line was my aria and I fucking milked it.

4th Innocent:
Io moi moi

In *Buffy the Vampire Slayer*, when Xander asks Spike why a blood ritual is required to open the gates of hell, he replies:

'Because it's always got to be blood. Blood is life. Why do you think we eat it? It's what keeps you going, makes you warm, makes you hard, makes you other than dead. Of course it's blood.'

Singing is about blood too. It might seem like it's about breath, about deep breaths and air pressure, and sure, that's important, but actually delivering the right amount of blood to the correct areas of the body as a note is hit is crucial. Blood is needed to swell the vocal chords, these two little purple curtains, these blood-rich little muscular folds that subconsciously shape the vowels. Blood is needed to work the lungs. So much blood is needed by the brain, that delicate and near-superhuman muscle, to process every remembered note, with all its related timbres, tempos and rhythms, and to cross-reference these with every real-time action made on stage. See, it's all about muscle memory. And muscles are powered by blood, by oxygenated blood, by gaseous transfer. Of course our need for blood and how our body copes and provides for this is entirely subconscious; breathing is the only outward and visible sign of these inner and intricate workings. Singing is a kind of sacrifice. Using your oxygen, your blood and all the delicate and inherent workings of your body to produce a note in those pressurised moments instead of prioritising just being alive. And as your body is doing this, working at full athletic capacity, you also have to follow the conductor and his gleaming baton. And this is to say nothing of the choreography. Every step taken on stage is rehearsed. And everything must look so natural, so real, even though you have no idea what a sacrificial victim lost deep in the blood-stained labyrinth might look like, feel or act.

Minotaur:
They bring
me these
gifts, these
innocents . . .
It seems to
me they are
chosen for
their beauty.
When I see
them I have
to spoil
them, these
creatures too
beautiful to
live, their
perfect
bodies, their
pale, soft
skin, my
image in
their eyes,
Asterios,
hideous,
reflected in
their eyes. I
pluck out
their eyes, of
course; I rip
their skin,
of course; I
foul their
bodies, of
course. They
bring me
these gifts of
blood . . .

4th Innocent: In the end Theseus kills the Minotaur. He's a hero, a kind
Olola . . . Io of Hercules-for-rent travelling from island to island. And
moi moi he has to. No matter how much self-knowledge and pathos is injected into a creature by the librettist and composer, someone who kills is dramatically on borrowed
time. Opera is sometimes fair like that. Sure, the innocent
die but their murderers, the monsters, are usually pun-
ished too. Unless of course the monster is society itself,
in which case there is no hero but time, and even time,
progress, is prone to failure. But the opera doesn't stop at
the last chord. Ovid tell us how Theseus' dad, thinking
his son eaten by the Minotaur, kills himself. He throws
himself off a cliff. Blood calls for blood.

4th Innocent: I remember when my voice broke and I couldn't go on
(in view) the choir trip to Wales. It was 1994 and I couldn't reach
Olola . . . the high B-flats needed for the solo, so Brendon Grace
suddenly got promoted from chorister to soloist. Brendon Grace was singing Fauré in Bangor Cathedral and
I was playing find-a-stone-throw-a-stone with my little
brother, digging up these gleaming quartzes that looked
like fragments of bone from the flowerbed in New
Malden. Six months later I became a countertenor. No
castration needed to sing the high notes, just a trick of
genetics, of blood.

It's hard to set a scream to music. Usually opera compos-ers don't ascribe pitch to such an utterance. Instead it is often written as a cross above the stave with a tail; the pitch is omitted and crossed out, the exact sounding left at the singer's discretion. Sometimes there is a little slop-ing slur next to the scream and this is the composer's way of indicating that it should descend. Sometimes this is ex-actly what the singer is doing, falling off a bridge or into hell or into the blood-stained passageways of a labyrinth.

The librettist–composer partnership between David Harsent and Harrison Birtwistle is a hugely successful one, possibly the most fertile and resonant within opera since Benjamin Britten and Myfanwy Piper produced *The Turn of the Screw* and *Death in Venice* together. It works for so many reasons – their shared understanding of dra-ma, their love of lyric poetry, their obsessions with folk-lore and myth – but it also functions on an elemental level. When asked why he worked with David Harsent so much, Birtwistle famously replied, 'David gives me what I need!' And that is words, words which can be set to music. No one can really set a scream, so Harsent found words for his sacrificial victims, his Innocents.

And these little words, these ancient phonetic utterances, suggest a melody. All speech does, but these tiny phrases are replete with little fallings, little deaths. *Olola. Io moi moi.* An *Oh* naturally falls in pitch as it is said, whereas an *Ah* or an *Ee* widens the mouth and complicates the linguistic descent. We did not go to our deaths willingly.

And what Birtwistle does with these tiny snatches of pain is miraculous. He plays with them. They become semiquavers, demisemiquavers and hemidemisemiquavers. They are like trills or cadences or ostinatos in the mouth. They are more alive than static. They seem not to be set at all. And this toying, this darkness, this sense of predator vs. prey in the very music, all of this came from Harsent's words.

The Minotaur is a unique opera for so many reasons, not least of all that it contains a new musical language for screams, for cries, for pain and for death throes.

4th Innocent:
(A war cry:)
Alalai—
alalai—
alalai

You might not know it from just listening but every phrase we Innocents sang brought us closer to the audience, closer to the Minotaur and closer to death. The libretto, with its stage directions, was a kind of map. *Closer. Closer still. In view. A response. A war cry. In death throes.*

4th Innocent:
(A war cry:)
Alalai—
alalai—
alalai

R: I am trying to write about *The Minotaur* and its libretto and was wondering if you could help me decode / translate the following phrases. *Olola. Io moi moi. Alalai – alalai – alalai.* D: Sure. *I am destroyed. Alas for me, for me. Alas, alas wanderings.*

4th Innocent:
(In their death throes, sing:)
Io-moi-moi . . .

No one teaches you how to die on stage. It is a kind of unmentioned thing in the rehearsal room and what little I ever knew I gleaned from watching the TV. I am not sure I ever really got it right; still, I tried to be subtle, un-hammy enough so that the director wouldn't mention me in their rehearsal notes and yet obvious enough so that the audience knew it was curtains. No one teaches you how to come back to life either. This is something that can sometimes happen in an opera. It never happened to me though, I always stayed dead.

SALLY BEAMISH

The Judas Passion

I knew David's work through his stunning libretti for Harrison Birtwistle, and had been mesmerised by his *Gawain* when I saw it in 2000. I once heard him speak at Warwick University, and have never forgotten his comments about being a librettist, and about working with Harry. I have often quoted him over the years. He bemoaned the lot of the librettist, the tweaks and cuts required, the lack of recognition; but at the same time one had a sense that he relished the role, even if it is, inexplicably, perceived as secondary in the annals of opera. What came over strongly was his delight in the ongoing collaboration with Harry. He described having to break it gently to him on several occasions that Harry had accidentally omitted setting several lines of text. ('How far back?' in a perfect imitation of Harry's Northern tones – an entertaining speciality of David's).

When David's name came up as a possible collaborator on *The Judas Passion*, the oratorio I had been commissioned to write for the Orchestra of the Age of Enlightenment, I leapt at the idea, and was delighted when he said yes.

We first met to discuss the piece in January 2016, and the conversation gathered more and more layers as we explored issues of spirituality, betrayal, destiny and faith. Was Judas evil? Or was he an instrument of the divine, without whom the salvific moment could not have happened?

David put a huge amount of thought and research into creating the libretto. Every now and then he would phone me, excited by a new discovery, a new connection. From the gnostic Gospel of Judas he seized on Jesus' startling words: 'You are the best of them. You will free me of the man that clothes me'. The idea of Jesus choosing Judas as his means of securing redemption for mankind became crucial to David's conception.

I received the beautifully paced, subtle and fascinating libretto in December 2016. The shapes and phrases lent themselves immediately to musical setting, and led me to musical colours I had never explored before. The music simply unfolded.

SIR HARRISON BIRTWISTLE

Interviewed by Nicola Nathan

In 1984, Harrison Birtwistle was on a train from Teddington to Waterloo; at the time he was Musical Director at the National Theatre and was on his way to work. He was reading the Sunday papers and came across a review, by Peter Porter, of David Harsent's book long sequence *Mister Punch*, in which Porter drew parallels between Harsent's book and Birtwistle's opera *Punch and Judy*. Birtwistle got the book and was sufficiently impressed by what he read to cold call Harsent and suggest a collaboration. When he answered the phone, Harsent wasn't sure who the caller was ('It's Harry Birtwistle here . . .') and almost hung up. The initial conversation went something like this:

'I wondered if you'd want to write an opera with me.'

'Yes, I would.'

'Don't you want to know what it's about?'

(Harsent had never written for the opera stage before and didn't understand that composers most often approached a librettist with a subject firmly in mind.)

'Oh, yes, sure . . .'

'Sir Gawain and the Green Knight.'

It was the beginning of a collaboration that has lasted until the present day. Birtwistle–Harsent pieces (described by the *New York Times* as 'an alchemically potent pairing') consist of two main-stage operas, two chamber operas, and three settings of projects arrived at after some discussion, though on one occasion, Birtwistle phoned Harsent and said, 'I need something . . . I've got a commission from the Nash Ensemble.' At the time, Harsent was working on *Marriage*, a collection that trades off the relationship between Pierre Bonnard and his mistress–model–wife, Marthe de Meligny, but also contains a sequence about the hare: a creature that is positively totemic in Harsent's work. Harsent said, 'You can either have the Martha/Mary division in women or the hare.' 'Right,' Birtwistle said, 'I'll have the hare.' *The Woman and the Hare* was subsequently performed at several London venues, at the Megaron in Athens and at Carnegie Hall.

When it comes to opera, Harsent and Birtwistle talk at length about before Harsent starts work. In a podcast made for the Royal Opera House in the run-up to the premiere of *The Minotaur*, Harsent remarked, 'If Harry and I had a dream about this piece, it would be a different version of the same dream.'

I interviewed Sir Harrison Birtwistle to get the composer's take on his librettist.

★

NN: *In what ways has David been significant to your creative life since you began your collaborations some thirty years ago?*

HB: David has helped me to realise certain of my dreams. Often the work is instigated by me: I have an idea and I mumble it out to him. It might be a one-word idea or an idea about a theatrical moment. When we did *The Corridor* all I knew was that the piece would be 'a moment'. With *The Minotaur* I had the notion of 'a bull' and with *Gawain* I wondered if it would be possible to stage someone's head coming off and for it to continue singing. From a compositional point of view, I consider a libretto to be a kind of dumbshow. What David has done for me is to realise those theatrical moments by providing me with a narrative for them.

For both song cycle and opera, since the words precede the music, would you say that David's texts necessarily impact on your compositional concerns?

I read a lot of poetry and I read it with a view as to how I might set it – some poems, some words, are completely unsettable. Though ultimately I can only be responsible for what a poem means to me, David gives me words that I know I can set.

The things that excite you or that interest you the most — are they the same things that excite and interest David? Would you say that the spaces you occupy creatively are the same spaces, or overlap with spaces, occupied by David?

That's a given — otherwise I wouldn't have him. There would be no point to our collaborations.

Take the question of myth. People often ask me why I set myth. First of all, that's not a question I have to answer, but if I were to answer it, I would say that a play or a piece of theatre about some modern psychological concern (say) doesn't have an atmosphere to which I can add. A modern text of this type isn't suitable for — doesn't need — music. I'm not interested in that kind of text.

It's not just a matter of matching or shared subject matter, interests or concerns. I'm very interested in the notion of distilled narrative. Take *Songs from the Same Earth*. After a while, David understood that what I wanted was a series of diverse poems about the same situation. It's not clear precisely what those poems are 'about'. And that's what interests me. It allows me to steal material from the poem and when I can steal from the poem, I know that's when there's something in it for me.

I'm interested in and choose to set poems that are distilled narrative because that verse — good verse — has a layer in which things are not absolutely clear, or it seems to me that the poem is about something more than itself. That's where the magic lies.

David is interested in the same thing — though I suspect he would refer to it as broken narrative.

Yes, broken narrative, hidden narrative, though I feel that the term 'distilled narrative' is a bit richer.

Let me put a notion in your head about music. Music has to exist in time; it has to begin and end and be a sequence in real time. But if you think back to a strand of music – any music – say, the National Anthem – when you think back to it, it is no longer in linear time but seems to be happening all at the same time.

Likewise, when I think back to getting those poems, it's as though I'd read a novel: a full linear narrative. I don't know exactly what the novel was about; perhaps a relationship that has fallen apart. I don't think David knows exactly what the hidden narrative is either. When I think of the songs now, I feel as though they are references to things, incidents, that are 'in the same package'. I wanted to write moments or sections from that imaginary novel that had their own musical identity. They are individual songs, characterised by their certain basic things like rhythm and speed. They relate to themselves musically but there's also a musical thread that runs through them and unifies them. Yet when I call them up in my head, I don't have each song in linear order, one after the other.

I think *Songs from the Same Earth* is the best thing I've done. Yes, I could have done something similar with somebody else, but it wouldn't then have been the same and I really like what it is. So it's not just the subject matter David and I share, it's a lot of different things. It has to be whatever floats your boat.

Do you have any plans for future collaboration?

Yes, a possible opera based around the fairytale of Jack and the Beanstalk and a piece that will arise from another existing collaboration, *The Woman and the Hare*.

LAVINIA SINGER

Essential Fragments:
the poems of In Secret *and* Salt

In a way, it was David Harsent's poetry that led to my first job in publishing. He was reading alongside Fiona Sampson at the first of the Poetry @ The Print Room series in Notting Hill, having recently published *In Secret: Versions of Yannis Ritsos*. Gripped, and so moved that I had to buy a copy, it was chatting while waiting for the sluggish PDQ machine to Stephen Stuart-Smith, the director at Enitharmon, that led to my working there for three years.

Harsent is staggeringly versatile, accomplished in numerous genres. Each project and collaboration seems to offer him an opportunity to experiment further, and, thrillingly, one cannot predict the nature of the next undertaking. But the particular qualities of the short and piercing lyric poems he read that night, heightened in the dark studio space, are just those shared in his most recent collection, *Salt*, published by Faber & Faber, where I work now. The two books therefore have a special resonance for me personally, but, on a wider level, they both capture an essence of Harsent's writing that makes it so compelling.

★

For *In Secret* Harsent selected the poems of Ritsos to translate that spoke to him most strongly, occasionally adapting them and their titles in his attempt to 're-imagine the piece, to test its pulse'.[1] The imagination is unmistakeably Harsentian, not only in setting and content, but also the mysterious methods by which he brings each piece to life.

---

1   *In Secret*, p. 79

...When night came on
we walked into town and happened to glance

through an open window. There they were,
man and wife, eating by lamplight. You could tell

everything from the way they dipped their heads,
unspeaking, and spooned their food.

Another man was standing at the table,
peeling an apple: slow turn of the knife ...

('Through the Window', *In Secret*)

In one room a man working, in another
a woman sitting still. Marriage bed, deathbed,
cold kitchen. Your guided tour of the house.
The staircase, the turn of the stair, a room kept dark.
Look in from outside: your shadow falls to the floor.

(p. 146, *Salt*)

In Secret and *Salt* both work through distillation. The poems, fragments in length and in their often-broken syntax, may present a scene *in media res* or a litany of objects, resembling a tableau or still life. Dramatic effect is created through glimpses, guess and gesture: 'You could tell / everything from the way they dipped their heads, / unspeaking'. To read, or to glance, is to enter a world of thresholds and twilight zones, often hinging on the prepositional: through a window, on the turn of the stair, at the edge of sleep. Experiences are reflected in mirrors or made strange by moonlight, and the result is to feel curiously disoriented – haunted, even. 'Dipped' heads, 'spooned' food: these simple words with their precise acoustic patterning – the scenes may be 'secret' or 'unspeaking' but rarely silent – demonstrate how impressive understatement can be.

In *Salt*, the poems are untitled; they are, as the author's note informs, a series that 'belong to each other in mood, in tone, and by way of certain images and words that form a ricochet of echoes'. The surround of white space – enhanced by the careful design and typesetting – means each image and word is weighed, granted an intensity that is highly potent.

At the book's launch, Harsent recommended what he considers to be the ideal method of reading the collection: one page per day, allowing space and time to let the words resonate. I tried this with the poem above. Relationships between the pairs and compounds – doublings and oppositions – develop flickeringly, simplifying and complicating by turns. The trios crescendo: bed, bed, kitchen; stair, stair, room. What is being revealed, and what 'kept dark'? There's a cunning handling of time, demonstrated in the blend of ongoing present action and closed-off past, which hovers between progress and stasis: does 'falls' in the last line bring resolution? The words here, as throughout the series, can play upon the mind in the form of meditation, riddle, or poison.

In both books, 'the mysteries of domesticity' – the tacit yet complex exchanges of everyday relationships – are subtly captured: slight movements, traces left after touching, a turned head or raised arm. A reader is unwittingly positioned as a kind of eavesdropper or scopophiliac, stumbling upon these private scenes, attempting to piece together and re-imagine the story. In this poetry, so much depends upon relations of power, and a great deal is handed to the unnamed, indeterminate 'you': the 'you' who glances, is granted a 'guided tour', and even, at times, participates or becomes implicated, 'your shadow falls to the floor'.

For tenderness is never far from menace. Measured monosyllables of a half-line may threaten deliberately: 'slow turn of the knife'. Intricately woven images beguile:

> The spider spins
> a gallows-tree
> of lace for the lacewing.

('XIX Tristichs', *In Secret*)

Harsent overtly references this poem in *Salt*, 'making use of' one of its lines on p. 172. The section quoted above is suggested in the compound noun 'spider-veins', listed as one of the 'signs of mortality' – which is exactly what the image, with its sibilant whispers, is. How insidious, the care exhibited in this small, creative yet deathly act, this nexus, this trap! The tristich form itself is a kind of loaded web; like the *Salt* poems set close to the centre of each page, untitled and monumental, the focused words acquire the significance of a sacrament or spell: 'a fragment of speech – something less / than half-said that carried its meaning entire' (p. 70).

'Meaning entire' – so much is meant, realms beyond the domestic. Local, habitual practices encapsulate universal rites of passage: 'Marriage bed, deathbed, / cold kitchen.' Each window and stair is Janus-faced, simultaneously pointing inwards and out, forwards and back. Classical figures and mythical stories are re-imagined, imbued with contemporary relevance and pathos. The backdrop of war punctuates *In Secret* in unambiguous outcry via gunfire, arrests, names on a list, a train taking soldiers to the front. *Salt* is shot through with visceral details characteristic of a crime scene: 'bad breath, smegma, spillage and swill . . . Broken glass, graffiti, blood . . . Dogshit, the bloom on rot'. Such substance, physical and raw, leaves an unpalatable aftertaste. The lonely, bare, desperate and vulnerable are presented unflinchingly – recognisable shades of the human condition. In all these ways, the poems capture what is essential.

★

Salt-flats of dream of memory of dream . . . limitless horizons
and out on the utmost rim (can you see?) a house
as white-on-white abstract except for the room-within-a-room
which can't be seen but can be known, white being one thing
in sunlight another under moonlight, not oblivion, not revival,
and the soul's song across that windless landscape, unheard;
by night the heart-stopped silence, by day the rising glare.

(p. 153, *Salt*)

You think you can second-guess your life
by reading the stars. What can I tell you? Tonight
things are as they are; tomorrow, who knows?

The moon throws a skitter-skim of light
on the waves, enough for you to see
the black boat coming in, that shadowy figure at the oars.

('The Black Boat', *In Secret*)

'The soul's song'; 'that shadowy figure'. 'A skitter-skim of light';
'the heart-stopped silence'. What can you see? What can be told?
Who knows. But I do think that these poems share essential
secrets, and that is one of the reasons to keep glancing through
and looking in. With Harsent as guide, the horizons are limitless.

Gawain

Gawain is still climbing through a city that is a forest filled with
    torn green air.
The buildings are trees streaming with hard glassy leaves,
and the roads are fast green rivers into which he stares,
and the ministries sprout dumb green tears.
The truth is that nature poetry is the only sort that anyone
    believes.

An axe cuts across the city and we call its bright edge the day.
A deer runs across the city and we call its green eyes woe.
Its hard green mouth opens to say
to you that there will be green hell to pay
the day when there is no more wilderness to go.

The wasteland inside Gawain has a hard green eye.
The city has lost its head which is still singing on.
The forest is a green axe that flies
out, and down through the night's dark green sky,
out and down across all that you do not fully understand is wrong.

Gawain is shooting through a camera made of grass and spores.
Gawain is howling with a voice made of a green spring.
Gawain is the world's least natural law.
Gawain is very sorry for his flaws.
Gawain is anything.

Nature became a highlights reel and then wildly ended.
Nature was always a really brilliant lie.
In what have we not offended?
Do you really want to know what your friend did?
Do you remember how deep it used to be to cry?

STEVEN GROARKE

Harsent and the Negative

From *A Violent Country* (1969) and *After Dark* (1973) through *Fire Songs* (2014), David Harsent's engagement with violent impulse represents one of the most vital contributions to English poetry over the last thirty-five years. The idea that 'There's no way back / through all that violence' (1973, p. 2) has continued to trouble the poet, but also to stir a remarkably wide-ranging thematic and stylistic response. Taken from an inaugural poem (the first poem in a volume dedicated to his father) entitled 'Two Postscripts to my Father', this stark formulation is emblematic of a contemporary worldview in which negation ('no way back') presents itself as a dilemma. The dilemma admits variations – including, most recently in *Salt*, the wish never to have come back at all (2017, p. 48); or the brute insistence that things simply cannot come back (2017, p. 61). And yet unlike the pathos of passing time, or the nostalgia of the *ubi sunt* motif ('Where are those who were before us?'), in which medieval Latin poetry provides a model for lamenting the transitory nature of all things, the past itself becomes a source of difficulty under the conditions of our modernity.

The contemporary poet is faced with this essential turn in the culture of value, where the pain (*algos*) associated with the way back, or the return (*nostos*), feels yet more pressing as the absolutely irrevocable becomes entangled with the scant hope of a voice calling us back (2017, p. 88). The modern tradition of Yeats and Eliot is defined by this particular sense of affliction (*tormentum*): tempted by a re-enactment of the myth of Orpheus, in which the legendary Thracian poet and musician turns to look at Euridice before they are both in the upper world and, thereby, causes her to vanish for good, the contemporary poet-heir, as Harsent (2017, p. 154) confirms, is summoned to look back the way he came. In Harsent (who isn't a visionary poet so much as an inveterate creative dreamer), this often involves a poem 'dreaming-back' something of the past that has yet to be experienced. The very seriousness of poetry, the full reach of its song, is at stake here. A *distressed* sense of the past, something in our temporal awareness that runs deeper than nostalgia, is a central part of what makes modern poetry feel difficult.

The difficulty remains more or less the same throughout Harsent's work; it consists in knowing how to confront something that has already happened. Harsent may seem too talkative a voice to fall apart, but I suggest that this is a reaction, a voluble defence against a breakdown that has already occurred (Winnicott, 1974). The breakdown is epitomised by the moment in 'Two Postscripts' 'when everything paused as you fell' (1973, p. 1). Harsent re-embodies this familiar occasion for poetry, with respect to the *fear of breakdown* that runs like a fault line through his poems, early and late, extending the reach for meaning from the parochial – the ordinary difficulties of daily living ('that cold house on the moor's edge'; 'We live / seven miles apart and seldom meet') – to the larger calamities and cataclysms of history.

I think these dark observations on the negative evidence of everyday life stand comparison with Larkin's thoroughly disenchanted worldview. I am not interested, here, in the question of influence so much as the allusive 'chain of echoes' (2017, p. 139) that may be found in Harsent's work, particularly with respect to the work of the negative.[1] Larkin is, I think, a significant figure in this associative chain. This is hardly a controversial point. Together, Larkin and Ted Hughes dominated English poetry in the 1960s

---

[1]   The 'work of the negative' (Green, 1999) includes destructive negativity, a type of mutilating psychic structure that negates life and obstructs growth, the clinical phenomenology of which was first set out by Melanie Klein. This forms part of a more comprehensive post-Freudian designation of the negative – including, repression, (*Verdrängung*), rejection (*Verwerfung*) or foreclosure (forclusion), negation (or disavowal), negative hallucination, blank pain, missing moments, the unlived life. Green extends the definition to include a potentially creative negative, drawing on Bion's (1970, p. 125) application of 'negative capability' as 'both prelude to action and itself a kind of action'.

and 1970s, and while not always a direct influence on later poets, nonetheless, their work 'provides signposts . . . for the strikingly different poetry which has succeeded them' (O'Brien, 1998, p. 23). Harsent is no exception, his work confirms the astuteness of O'Brien's evaluation. And it is important to note, for our purposes, that the legacy of Larkin is heretical not simply because it reminds us that we have to die in a universe without grace (a secular *memento mori*); but also, on account of what O'Brien (1998, p. 28) in commenting on 'Afternoons' defines as its 'imperfectly explained pessimism'. The poem creates this situation, where *something comes to nothing* in the ruinous winds. Paradoxically, the judgement of the negative appears both vague and formidably certain here. There is in fact something of a craving for certainty that isn't always immediately obvious in Larkin, although the mood of washed-out despair is captured more emphatically in (for example) 'Going, Going' – with the unequivocal announcement 'And that will be England gone'.

Larkin's 'stripped standard English voice', characteristically 'held in check by the quotidian' (Heaney, 1976, p. 165), sets the tone for the idea that there is 'no way back' from a disaster that has already happened. Larkin addresses this anxiety primarily as a matter of aging. I don't think there is any reason to assume that Harsent shares Larkin's preoccupation with *aging*. Nevertheless, the idea that there is 'no way back' echoes the wider sense of annulment and ruin that lies at the heart of much of Larkin's poetry. No English poet since Larkin, I suggest, has proved himself more available than Harsent to the ruinous figure of 'wrong beginnings' and the concomitant anxiety that living comes to nothing. The claim appears in *Dreams of the Dead*: 'There was nothing to hear or touch; / there was nothing to be kept' (1977, p. 32), and is repeated twice in *Night*: 'nothing returns or renews' (2011, p. 13); 'nothing repairs or restores' (2011, p. 65). It is repeated again in *Salt*, explicitly, as a failure of language and listening: 'Nothing abides, no, and nothing prospers' (2017, p. 139). A clear sense of the primordial corruption of human nature in both poet, albeit expressed in decidedly non-metaphysical terms, underwrites the 'depth of darkness', which, as Harsent describes it in 'Night', reaches 'Black actuality' in the movement between disaster and anxiety. And the devastating rhyming couplets of 'Necrophilia' confirm the brute judgement of negation: 'No wayward promise, nothing to shake the heart, / nothing to warm to, no trace of harm or hurt' (2011, p. 67). The further rhyme of 'bliss' with 'kiss' underscores the sexual morbidity of nihilism as a permanent risk.

Harsent (2017) proposes the associative 'chain' as a method for his own poetry. Equally, it defines the reach for meaning at work in the wider response of contemporary English poetry to the negative. To take Larkin again. The nihilating effect of 'unresting', 'afresh' and 'dead' – i.e., in the transposition from 'The Trees' to 'Aubade' (Heaney, 1990, pp. 155-6) – issues unabashed from the perspective of self-sufficient humanism. Negative pressure expresses itself as a type of arrogance, which cancels the last remnants of a reparative urge in the English culture of churchgoing.[2] The negative, in other words, is rendered as necessity (*Ananke*), a negating drive in the order of things, the moral significance of which is evident in Larkin's acceptance of what Heaney (1990, p. 159) calls 'the ultimate bleakness of things'. Negation is reckoned as a fundamental principle of reality, if not the basic assumption of an entire *Weltanschauung*. And looked at in the wider context of cultural values, this assessment of disciplining reality confirms something that belongs by way of substitution to what Freud (1925, p. 239) called the 'death drive' (*Todestriebe*) or the 'instinct

---

2   Cf. C. H. Sisson (1993), who was no less harsh or sceptical than Larkin (both poets were inclined to lash out), for an alternative measure of Anglican-ism in the context of the darker mysteries of religion. Sisson's rigorous Tory approach to the matter of England, and the Church of England, sets him apart from the mainstream of Larkin and Hughes, and suggests an alternative series of deep echoes, with respect to the modern negative in English poetry – 'There is not Nothing if not I / For 'I' is only emptiness. / And what comes flooding in. The Time, / The Place: the Matter, nothing less' (cf. 'The Matter' from his 1980 collection *Exactions*). Harsent manages something comparable to this only in his most recent work.

of destruction'. Mallarmé's '*l'éternal azur*' is thus turned by a 'scrupulous meanness' (Heaney, 1976, p. 164), which is at work in Larkin's attitude towards life, into the manifest 'no' of reality – 'endless' as well as 'nothing' and 'nowhere' (cf. 'High Windows'). In a typically understated attempt to settle the modern reader into the perception of negation as a figure of necessity, Larkin proposes that the 'mind blanks' without end. Harsent, in turn, renders negative pressure, if not the negating drive, in the mirror image of 'a depthless blank / of sky' (2011, p. 5).

★

To underline the Shakespearean reach involved in the work of the negative, Harsent intensifies matters in *Salt* by rendering the adjective ('blank') or the noun ('blankness') as a verb in the opening phrase 'His mirror image blanked him' (2017, p. 56). The paradoxical nature of the work is yet more explicit in the idea of a world gone 'blank with waiting' (2017, p. 175), where the not-yet-conceived issues from so many blank expectations. What are we waiting for? Is there any point in our doing so? Tellingly (although the manoeuvre isn't necessarily typical of the poet), Hughes, in his poem 'Pibroch', settles matters in the vernacular; bearing witness to the elemental – i.e., the 'meaningless voice' of the sea, the 'black sleep' of the created world, and the wind's ability 'to mingle with nothing' – the poem meets the prospect of indifferent nature with apparent confidence. A mind that has 'gone completely' reflects a deeper boredom with 'the appearance of heaven'; an indifference in both cases that, albeit in different ways, signifies beyond cruelty.

This remains a pre-eminent example of the use of violence in English poetry since the Second World War. By contrast, Harsent and Larkin tend to rework blankness as a complex function of the negative, where the image *draws a blank*. At the same time, 'the Daughters of Necessity' (2011, p. 3) forge a link between two of the most persistently unillusioned English poets of the past half-century. We would, I suspect, have to go back to Hardy (Larkin's claim on his mentor's unalloyed sadness, rather than the remnants of his belief), or to certain passages in Edward Thomas, for a comparable collapse of illusion in recent English poetry.

I shall come back, intermittently, to the comparison with Hughes and the matter of dark energies; it is clearly an indispensable part of the chain that links Harsent to the deep echoes of the modern English negative. But, for our purposes at least, Heaney's comparative reading of Larkin and Yeats is probably more illuminating. The comparison itself is instructive. But it doesn't allow for the possibility that the negative situation operates, through the immanent admixture of instinctual drives, as a composite figure of negativism and affirmation. Given the fact that life issues out of terrible things (Yeats's 'terrible beauty'), my proposal is that *poetic affirmation admits the negative*, that renewal presupposes a disaster that has yet to be experienced.

This is a matter of some import when it comes to Harsent. Without wishing to reduce things to a straightforward resolution, I think the irreducible *fusion* of Eros and aggression does in fact become increasingly evident in his work. The use of the verb 'blanked' makes the point. It attributes action to the 'missing moments' of an unlived life, mixing the active and the passive, and rendering erasure itself as an indissoluble work of the negative. It isn't necessarily a case of irrevocable loss. The notion of 'missing moments' suggests that something should have happened but did not, that one is left to make sense of what has been blanked.

Neither one of Heaney's alternatives fits here. In fact, Harsent's work resonates with elements from the traditions of both Yeats and Larkin, and I don't think our understanding of his poetry is helped much by the dualism of Freud's final instinct theory any more than the binary opposition of negative evidence and affirmative impulse in Heaney.

Essentially, it is the action or work of *mixing* (at the level of language) that I wish to emphasise, particularly the construction and affirmation of meaning on negative ground. In contrast to the figure of necessity, which is marked exclusively by the 'vindictive force' of mere negation (cruelty), Harsent admits a much wider field of operation under the heading of the negative – most notably, what he describes in 'Cockade' as 'the missing moments in our lives' (1973, p. 11). He certainly doesn't play down the prevalence of human cruelty, or promise an easily reconciled life. As part of his remarkably comprehensive response as a poet, he credits the moment when everything stands in the negative. And yet 'missing moments' promise more than the catastrophic disillusionment expressed in the psychotic fear of breakdown. We don't go to Harsent, as we might to David Jones or Geoffrey Hill, for the *ecclesia* of prayer; closer in this respect (once again) to Edward Thomas, Harsent recalls the 'stark repetitions of prayer' (2017, p. 74) in a world without grace.

I think this point is worth noting. The commonweal is increasingly absent from our habits of language; for all its social and governmental settlements, contemporary speech rarely gravitates to the vocation of assembly. In this context, we turn to poetry in order to renew our sense of negative capability. Thus the 'repetitions of prayer', which Harsent places more or less at the centre of *Salt*, offer a 'stark' reminder of something that isn't there; together with the remnants of liturgy, prayerful repetitions add to the indelible afterimage of faith. The spectre of riddance notwithstanding, 'missing moments' and the 'repetitions of prayer' augment the reach for meaning beyond the concrete manifestations of annulment, but also in the direction of transcendence. They create an afterlight. It isn't only so-called religious poets who imbue the language with an answering pressure. Harsent takes a further step on Larkin's 'serious earth' (cf. 'Church Going'), where the act of drawing a blank – indeed, Larkin's image of a 'mind' engaged in its own blanking or purgation – may yet exceed the state of blankness, even if faith tends to express itself on the 'spur of the moment'. Harsent counts the deceived among 'the true obsessives' (1977, p. 51) – but while we aren't deceived by either poet: life's end is death; nonetheless, disillusionment admits various possibilities.

★

To come back to 'Two Postscripts', while the poem contains a disturbing impression of violent encounter, it also includes the question of how one might actually begin 'to piece it all together' (1973, p. 1). The poem manages to gather sufficient imaginative resources by the very act of naming the 'no'. As a foundational example of the active absence that enlivens Harsent's negative, the poem offers what we might call a disillusioned afterimage, which is a *piecing together* of sorts, something written after all that has happened, even after everything has fallen apart. Structurally, the poem unfolds through a subtle use of supplementary logic, with the alternating rhythm of 'love' and 'pain' set out some twenty-five years after the violent contraction of the world depicted in the first of the poem's two parts. The catastrophe concerns a world drawn inward and concentrated around a core of pain, which is then repeated here-and-now – with so many photographic images of an earlier life scattered on the desk before the poet. The visible world is central to Harsent's poetry, although he approaches visibility in different ways across the course of his work. To begin with, the imagery is routinely spare and crystalline in contrast to the later work, where it tends to heap up, with images feeding on images in associative stacks. In *Salt*, the dense network of imagery breaks up once more into an extraordinary series of distilled fragments.

In 'Two Postscripts', then, the imagery is parred back – the 'roar', the 'sudden heat', the 'acres of sky' and the 'splash of blood'; further to which the photographs form an integral part of the 'aftershock'. As for the drama of the poem, the breakdown that has already occurred is transmitted, retrospectively, from one generation to the next. Addressed to a living father, albeit in anxious anticipation of the dead father and all that destroys life, the *postscrĩptum* constitutes part of the groundwork for Harsent's subsequent and varied attempts to *write afterwards*.[3] The retrospective logic of renewal or restoration applies to any work of art, insofar as it 'obliges us to think the actuality of pain . . . which means thinking what generates pain . . . rather than lamenting its inevitability' (Williams, 2016, p. 75). The bleakest of works presupposes a generative force; but there are nonetheless different ways of handling the universals of pain and death. Larkin emphasises the *fact* of pain; whereas Hughes tends to play up the dark energies of 'the northern deposits' (Heaney, 1976, p. 151), arguably, to the point of nihilism in *Crow*.

Harsent offers a further alternative in which 'black actuality', the radically nihilating contraction of inner and outer worlds, is consistently offset by the manifestation of life coming into its own. Although a ruthless satirist at times, he doesn't limit the negative to a mood of worldly cynicism or unyielding irony. On the contrary, the violent breakthrough of creative negativity is evident (once again) in the 'stark repetitions of prayer' – indeed, in 'Punch's Day Book' prayer figures as 'the almost-possible' (1984, p. 62). Central to what Green (1999, p. 138) sees as 'the fecundity of the negative', the almost-possible demarcates what 'can only be understood in the light of a future which has not yet occurred, and, which is never really recognisable in what is but only allusively in its potential for prefiguration'. The martyr is a paradigmatic figure of this allusive future-to-come. Historically, global terror has redefined the context of modern witness, the figure of potentiality, and the extremes to which people are prepared to go in the name of belief.

Harsent, for his part, brings these questions sharply into

---

3   Compare Vendler (1998) on Heaney's 'afterward', the incorporation of first thoughts into second thoughts, typically, in sequences that reflect the aftermath of Northern Ireland's quarter-century of civil unrest. Vendler renders 'afterwards' as a question of endurance, which she applies to the extended uses that Heaney makes of the lyric under pressure. As such, the question is especially relevant for our theme: 'How can one "say" stoicism in form?'

focus: the contraction of martyrdom, which he later reworks to devastating effect in *Fire Songs*, yields a sign of promise in *Mister Punch*, precisely in the aftermath of the most terrible rages. The sacramental life itself is subject to reclamation, where violence – 'A slip of the blade' (1984, p. 22) – has run amok. And yet however extreme things have become, we are encouraged to keep faith with life on the primordial grounds of 'negativisation' (*la négativation*) and excess (Green, 1999, p. 12). Harsent makes something of these inherent aspects of psychic life, most notably, in the form of missing moments and the unlived life. Garnering missing moments presupposes a type of poetic 'working-through' (*Durcharbeitung*), and Harsent assumes this task (with due pathos) in 'After Dark' – 'I close my eyes / and invent arrivals' (1973, p. 3).

Violence marks the beginning of pain, as we have seen in 'Two Postscripts', with respect to a breakdown that has already occurred: 'The world . . . / shrank to a splash of blood as the pain began' (1973, p. 1). It is only with the invention of a future (*avenir*), the sense of a coming (or advent), or a sign of promise, that the disaster may be experienced in the past tense. Writing afterward thus provides a framework in which pain can be suffered, and in which the martyr achieves something more than an empty repetition or mere negation.

★

Pain, as Harsent puts it in *Salt*, has 'its own palette' (2017, p. 10); analogous to the work of the word, painful affect alternately unpicks us and pieces us together. We are inevitably unravelled by painful experience. But poetry attends to what pain does *not* take away. This, at least, is what I think Heaney means when he refers to the 'redressal' of poetry; it forms part of his own lyric use of the 'afterward'. In the most 'original' and 'illuminating' poetry, according to Heaney (1990, pp. 159-60), the work comprises a difficult encounter with 'the limitations of human existence itself' and with our limiting knowledge: 'The knowledge is limiting because it concedes that pain necessarily accompanies the cycles of life'. As the case of the martyr demonstrates, this is of course an historical as well as an ontological proposition.

The modern negative, which encompasses the gamut from Yeats to Larkin, is inevitably subject to the cessation of growth. The canonical instance of which, in twentieth-century English poetry, appears in Eliot's recoil from the rejuvenation of April, the life-denying opening phrase of *The Waste Land*. And yet the same holds for Eliot as for Harsent: the *stasis* of negation – which is given in Harsent's rhyme of 'pain' with 'freeze-frame' (2011, p. 66) or in 'stopless silence' as the image of accumulated loss (2017, p. 24) – is nonetheless set against a series of potentially restorative images – Eliot's 'breeding', 'mixing', 'stirring' and 'feeding'. Suffering and death stand on fecund ground (cf. the image of 'birthblood' in 'The Woman and the Rooks'), where poetry continues to work through the limits, channelling the dark energies of violent impulse, and thereby preserving human freedom against a too-certain knowledge of annulment and failure.

But what does the work involve? How does poetry credit what pain does not take away? The question of efficient form draws attention to an important distinction, particularly in the art of modern poetry, regarding self-revelation and the self-affectation of sensibility. The infamous controversy in American criticism, during the 1950s, over so-called confessional poetry (Rosenthal, 1960), consolidated the distinction between these two types of poetic response: the expression of typically shameful personal confidences on the one hand and, on the other, a reticent, impersonal attitude combined with formal precision and a characteristically severe style. We would want to be able to differentiate between (say) Sylvia Plath and Thom Gunn.[4] And yet it's a moot point whether

---

4   The notion of self-expression was anathema to Gunn, whose private remarks on Plath were nonetheless characteristically nuanced (Wilmer, 2017, p. XLI). Taken together with his impeccable handling of form, Gunn's delicate evocation of affect without hysteria sets him apart from the majority of his peers.

we require the criterion of 'confession' in order to do so, let alone the extravagant panoply of Alvarez (1966) on the fate of poetry in England during the immediate post-war period. Ultimately, it seems to me the binary opposition holds up no better here than it does in the case of Yeats and Larkin. And again, Harsent proves himself centrally resistant to the dichotomy, presenting a poetry grounded in affect, animistic in places, and adequate to the demands of so-called 'extreme' experience. At the same time, however, his poetry achieves something of an 'impersonal' touch through the formal play of masks, personae, voice and irony. The autobiographical feel of a Harsent poem is seldom straightforward; in fact, as he puts it himself, his poems rely for the most part on 'little fictions'. 'Elsewhere', the final long poem in *Night*, is a fine example of his ability to handle, without recourse to confession, the often-precarious balance between negativism and affirmation.

Harsent shares something of Gunn's preoccupation with the irreducible sensation of feeling and the potentialities of affect, allowing for the fact that the inner workings of renewal presuppose deep-seated recognition of the world of concrete sensation. The chain of echoes, which Harsent claims self-consciously as a method, encompasses the rhythm and melodies rooted in an underlying babble (one's mother tongue) as well as the many voices of the historical and immemorial past. But to ground the work in feeling and experience, sounding out and giving shape to the echoing rhythms of an ancestral negative, doesn't necessarily involve the *confession* of pain. For Harsent, as for Eliot, pain and failure persist, under the sentimental conditions of our modernity, as *forms of difficulty*. Most notably, *The Waste Land* and *Mister Punch* (Harsent's indisputably major poem) offer alternative mythopoeic patterns of post-tragic consciousness and its defining difficulties.

Briefly, Eliot gave voice to a historic situation in the interwar years, when the ground appeared to have been laid to waste, reduced to no more than a heap of fragments ('broken images'), even as

Augustine's wanderer became unto himself a waste or barren land.[5] Cast in a defiant mood of catastrophic disillusionment, much of the poem comprises the memories of Tiresias, arguably the poem's central persona, as the Fisher King marked by his failure with the Grail-bearer in the Hyacinth garden (cf. 'The Burial of the Dead'). The sacramental Grail mystery shapes the meaning that Eliot's poem gives to failure, to the sterility of a 'love' that has turned away from marriage and towards lust, but also to the possibility of redemption and its potential for prefiguration. Here, as elsewhere, Eliot confirms our basic predicament in terms of the search for an *active* correlative that may yet prove beyond us.

★

Similarly, in *Mister Punch* Harsent invents a persona that bears witness to the calamities of our post-tragic lives. His interior view, however, is anything but an occasion for personal confession or self-revelation. Instead, it reveals a complex associative chain of images, comprising memory-images, sensory images and verbal images. A detailed exegesis of *Mister Punch* isn't possible here. Suffice to note that Harsent consistently turns even his most intimate poetry towards the world and its systems of meaning. For example, 'Marriage' – which, at one point, renders domesticity 'Next to nothing' (2002, p. 30) – is the most sustained instance of a characteristic laying open of interiority and its privacies to a wider world of meaning. Here, the poem is turned outward, the inside is exposed as an inner work of meaning, particularly with respect to the modernity of looking. Most importantly, the handling of intimacy in 'Marriage' relies on an uncompromising measure of 'the deepening / aftershock' (2002, p. 34).

And the sequence raises a question that repeats itself with a degree of urgency in *Salt* – 'Does this image come back to

---

5   'But I deserted you, my God. In my youth I wandered away, too far from your sustaining hand, and created of myself a barren waste' (*Confessions*, II, x).

you as it does to me?' (2017, p. 161). The question of 'coming back' is indissociably linked to the question of images. This is a fundamental link and one that Freud (1915, p. 201) underlined in his metapsychological paper 'The Unconscious': 'the presentation of the *thing* . . . consists in the cathexis, if not of the direct memory-images of the thing, at least of remoter memory-traces derived from these'. Looked at from the perspective of writing afterwards, Freud identifies the general topographical schema in which (a) the 'memory-trace' (*Erinnerungsspur*) registers impressions of the event; (b) the 'thing-presentation' (*Dingvorstellung*) reactivates and revitalises the memory-trace; and (c) the conscious presentation presupposes a combination of the pre-verbal presentation of the thing (essentially visual) with the 'word-presentation' (*Wortvorstellung*) or verbal linguistic symbol.

While Eliot raised much the same question in terms of the 'objective correlative', the Freudian schema provides a useful model for the deep echoes of associative chains – including, the archaic perception of pain and its poetic representation. In a culture where the right to happiness invariably becomes a duty to achieve it (Pontails, 1977), we turn to poets for vital images of pain, painful witness and painful experience. Williams defines the use we make of the tragic imagination in these terms. And I think Harsent insists on meeting this need with all the stylistic resources at his command. The early poems are replete with extremes of emotional pain – the madness of Nijinsky and of the Syriac ascetic saint Simeon Stylites; the realisation of an anticipated literary memorial in the case of a suicide; and repeated depictions of violent death. But Harsent isn't in any meaningful sense of the word a 'psychological' poet. If Heaney (1976, p. 158) is right in his surmise that Ted Hughes is primarily intent on making vocal the inner life – then, at bottom, the northern poet is engaged in a very different kind of work to that of Harsent. We are grateful to Heaney for drawing our attention to different uses of the Anglo-Saxon base. Thus, Harsent presents what we might call *styles* of psychic pain, rendering the experience of pain through various stylistic means, more often than not, on the threshold of language and its achievements. At its most cutting, his work echoes a scholastic tradition of English poetry in which style, including the manner of setting down and piecing together, is inseparable from the convictions, if not the faith it affects (Hill, 2003).

The exigency of pain is felt through the irreducible combination of style and conviction. Again, this doesn't necessarily involve a confessional mode, although personal style, the idiomatic impression that the poet leaves in the language, is a matter of first importance. As for his own style of faith, Harsent is especially forthright when it comes to negation as a symbol. While he may be counted, together with Larkin and the vast majority of his own generation, among the many voices of post-Christian English poetry, his symbolism is nonetheless subject to the 'heartbeat rhythms of prayer' (2011, p. 65). We are left in no doubt that negation belongs to language. Thus, admitting the 'residue of prayer' (2011, p. 30) that falls upon our lips, indeed as a sign of the coming of God to mind (*la venue de Dieu à l'idée*), Harsent assumes the defining difficult of his work in the phrase 'after dark'. The symbolic import of the latter draws attention to the 'aftershock', understood as a repeated reenactment, in increasingly greater depth, of an absolute pain.[6]

★

The imaginative depth of Harsent's poetry becomes increasingly apparent with the inclusion of archetypes, folk and ballad traditions,

---

6   Pontalis (1977) differentiates neurotic forms of separation anxiety from a blank, primordial agony, which, he suggests, may be seen in Lacan's '*la douleur d'exister*'. Tustin (1972) offers an alternative clinical account of these primitive existential agonies, which she relates to the premature experience of separateness from the maternal body at the beginning of life. She describes this fundamental trauma as a 'black hole' experience, the phenomenology of which is first set out in the case of a three-year-old boy. I argue below that we can compare this type of primitive agony to Harsent's treatment of the martyr in *Fire Songs*.

personae and myths, alongside the effective use of dramatic sequences, and, most recently in *Salt* (2017), a series held together by the associative play of 'disjointed narratives', 'echoes' and a distinct 'emotional climate' or 'mood'. Harsent is, in many ways, a difficult poet to place, which is indicative of the independence, if not the eccentricity of his style. Nevertheless, the question of inheritance persists in important and fundamental ways, and it seems to me that Harsent's distinctive reworking of the negative reveals the scope of his debt. This includes his debt to Yeats as the central modern poet.

The poet proves himself adequate to his task even as he admits his own destructiveness. And Harsent demonstrates the truth of this claim in a highly condensed image of negation after Yeats and the rape of Leda. Collected in *A Violent Country*, this extraordinary tercet encapsulates the laying open of intimacy to a world of meaning. Yeats (1925/2008, p. 176) himself is uncompromisingly extremist in his range of associations: 'I imagine new races . . . seeking domination, a world resembling but for its immensity that of the Greek tribes – each with its own *Daimon* or ancestral hero – the brood of Leda, War and Love; history grown symbolic, the biography changed into a myth'. In effect, Harsent's work includes a series of reworkings on this basic pattern of violent impulse, which, in galley proofs of *A Vision*, explicitly identifies every 'act of war' as an 'act of creation', counting life itself as a preparation for war.

The most likely pictorial source of Yeats's sonnet remains a matter of literary-critical debate. Nevertheless, we can I think count Michelangelo's 'Leda and the Swan', which dates from 1530 but is only extant itself in copies and variants, among the many representations of the mythic scene, ranging from Ovid to the Italian Renaissance. And so long as the original image is missing, this only heightens the sense of Harsent's poem as an *afterimage*. The contemporary poet, like the post-oedipal subject of Freudian metapsychology, is always a latecomer at the scene of sexual violence. The poet inherits a sense of guilt modelled on an identification with the violence of the father (Zeus in the myth) in the primal scene, which Yeats reimagines as the terror and sweetness of tribal solitude. Further elaborations on the afterimage of sexual violence, repeated throughout Harsent's work, are brought to a pitch in *Mister Punch*. In this respect, the same is true for Harsent as for Yeats: the trauma of the primal scene (*Urszene*) – *i.e.*, the sexual intercourse between the parents – isn't confined to a psychological frame of reference. Folk-memory, 'something primordial' (1984, p. 13), plays a significant part in the case of *Mister Punch*. Yeats works comparable seams in Celtic myth, faery lore, and the spirit world. But 'Leda and the Swan', as Longley (2013, p. 117) states incisively, is also 'the ultimate heretical war sonnet'.

The belatedness of writing afterwards is integral to the contemporary poet's historic sense of guilt. In this respect, the violence alluded to in Harsent's poem 'Leda' – including the shocking image of the girl's acquiescence ('loosening thighs') and her possible glorying in the power of the gods – takes place elsewhere. The same applies to the lapse of twenty-five years in 'Two Postscripts'. The fear of a disaster that has already taken place, in both historical and mythological terms, is an integral part of the anxiety. It forms part of the poet's identity and definition *as heir*; hence the oedipal scene of writing afterwards as a twofold dilemma of style and conviction. In 'Leda', the darkness and the violence, or the terror and the sweetness, are located not only in Yeats (whose poem dates from the 1920s) as the pre-eminent voice in modern poetry; but also, in the primordial destructiveness of classical mythology. The sestet recalls the destruction caused by Leda's progeny ('the brood of Leda'), Helen and Polydeuces, as well as the taint of her mother's rape in Clytemnestra; it stands witness to the mythical events that unfold in the aftermath of the rape – the birth of Helen, the Trojan War, and the murder of Agamemnon.

The Trojan war and the mythological image of parricide stand in back of both the Leda poems. Consequently, as the contemporary poet-heir, Harsent is subject to an anxiety over something that has already happened in the immemorial past. His poem reworks violent impulse as a singular afterimage: 'Her thighs damp with his drool' (1969, p. 5). The negative continues to exert itself in this way as a pressure of renewal, reinvention and reclamation – *i.e.*, a reworking of classical mythology after Yeats. The contemporary poet's image of lascivious, immoderate pleasure ('drool'), the inordinate lengths to which Harsent is bound to go in staking his claim on the cultural imaginary, reflects Yeats's own preoccupation with primary creativity as a type of destructiveness (the engendering shudder in the loins) alongside the theme of mythical copulation with animals. In more ways than one, Harsent's violated woman appears *afterwards*, sticky with the absent presence of violence. As such, she appears in stark contrast to the Goddess from the garden sequence in *Night*, where 'the dab of cuckoo-spit / that fell to her thigh' leaves 'a trickle of glisten' that the woman herself describes as 'slick, like a scar in velvet' (2011, pp. 14-5). The Garden Goddess appropriates the image of her own sexuality with authority; whereas Harsent's Leda appears altogether less sure of herself, less confident, and more wanting in panache. She is in fact among the first in a series of isolated female figures in Harsent. Turned (as the tercet itself turns) in the unspecified sentiment of her gaze, she goes on searching her own reflection for what the encounter has made of her, even as the poem itself appears as an anxious, broken reflection of 'Leda and the Swan'.

★

To take a final example, the first of the four 'Fire' poems, from *Fire Songs*, demonstrates Harsent's distinctive contribution to the answering pressure of the negative. It is one of his finest poems. Set against the historical background of Tudor England and its religious turmoil, the martyrdom of Anne Askew (1521-46) marks a harrowing trajectory from extreme violence to the transformation of a gift. There is no avoiding the horror. Askew was taken to the

Tower of London in 1546, where she remained 'wordless under torture' (2014, p. 3), before being burned at the stake for heresy. Harsent doesn't spare his readers. The visceral brutality of the final scene at Smithfield, London, is imagined without reserve: 'My dream of her puts me in close-by . . . as she browns from heel / to head, as she cracks and splits' (2014, p. 6). The figure of heresy is overdetermined by a scandalous association in 'Vanitas' that recalls Yeats's extremist attitude – namely, the coming together of the tyrant and martyr *in joy*.

This is the afterimage as closeup, where the nearness of violence is essential to the way back and, therefore, to the possibility of making sense of things. Ted Hughes aims at a comparable effect, between the 'blank' and 'printed' page, in his own emblematic and inaugural poem 'The Thought-Fox'. In a strong reading of the sexual-linguistic trajectory from 'Something more near / Though deeper within darkness' to 'the dark hole of the head', Heaney (1976, p. 154) traces the triumph of the monosyllabic consonants over the anarchic lusciousness of the vowels. The distinctive Hughesian boast is on full display in this poem. For Harsent, as for Hughes, it is the very violence, at the point of entry, that makes it possible to piece it all together on the page, even when faced with 'fire and flesh that nobody can own' (1977, p. 36). The poet's obligation to bear witness, here, overrides any thoughts of redemption.

Harsent uses similar means to remarkable effect in rendering the blankness of war in *Legion* – indeed, where it often appears as if 'there's nothing to be said' (2005, p. 37). And elsewhere in the same volume, the trope of blankness (blank pain, blank page) again places the negative 'close-by' – 'I have come to come / to nothing, or less than nothing if nothing / is absence' (2005, p. 53). Where there is pain, the evocation of nothingness is invariably in play; and the central question here, reprinted in Harsent's versions of Ritsos, concerns the paradox of an absent presence – 'something, or nothing at all?' (2005, p. 69; 2012, p. 52). Once again, the fusion of seemingly irreconcilable formal elements gives us the violent impulse at its most intense and variegated. On the one hand, Harsent inherits a primal scene that evokes the sense of 'something else' alive and near (Freud's thing-presentation); on the other hand, the tristich, favoured by the Greek poet, provides an appropriately spare, stripped back form for the evocation of nothingness. Both gestures occupy a central place in Harsent's work.

Meanwhile, the first of the 'Fire' songs quotes from the record: '*sylence alwayes her gift*' (2014, p. 3). The poet relies on a vocative intimacy – 'Anne, you are nothing to me' (2014, p. 4) – in conjunction with an allusion to *King Lear* and Cordelia's speechless love: 'What shall Cordelia speak? Love, and be silent' (I. i. 61). As with 'Leda', the figure of a woman isolated by violence appears at the centre of the poem. This prompts a final comparison with Yeats. Harsent's Leda is left alone to search her reflection, even as Yeats would have her reflect on the complicity of her desire.

And yet for Anne Askew, as for Cordelia, it is more a question of standing by what cannot be said – through the figure of apophasis in Cordelia's case – to the point of death. The vocative 'You are nothing to me' comes into play on the grounds of faith, and as such functions as the condition of an afterimage, rather than the *terminus ad quem* of the negative. The image is harrowing, rather than desolate. Shakespeare provides the model, here, for the inner work of piecing together as an 'impersonal' inward touch. Harsent's poem thus works through an irrevocable historic disaster and, in retrospect, combines excerpts from the record (the archive of pain) with contemporary associations to the martyr's silent witness. We are by now familiar with the defining dilemma – 'as if music might break the silence, or silence be endless' (2017, p. 176). In the meantime, the rhyme of 'pain' and 'freeze-frame' is burst asunder by the 'yes' that comes back to the poet-heir (Anne Askew was also a writer and poet, indeed one of the earliest-known female poets to compose in the English language) through the fire – '*yes, it will be fire it will be fire it will be fire . . .*'

KATE KELLAWAY

Night: *A Review*

First published in the *Guardian*, Sunday 13 February, 2011

David Harsent's tenth collection can be read almost like a novel in that most of the poems belong to a continuing world. In other ways, this could not be less like a novel. It demands re-reading. The experience is like setting out on a journey at night: your eyes take time to get used to the dark. These are among the most frightening poems I have ever read. It does not come as a surprise to learn that Harsent once wrote crime fiction. But it would be misleading to say his poems are frightening in the way a thriller is. They are far more enigmatic, unburdened by plotty reassurances and free of resolutions. Harsent creates a suspense that has no ending. His poems have something in common with the novels of John Banville – especially *The Book of Evidence* – in that they describe a world charged with emotion, stained with shame, in which nothing is neutral and where lyricism thrives but can never absolve. As in all the worst nightmares, even the light turns out to be frightening.

The narrator has evicted himself from his former life. In the opening poem, 'Rota Fortunae', he writes: '. . . and there floods in, now as never before, that sense / of giving yourself over to chance / that will turn you for home, or take you to the brink'. By the last poem, the sun has taken fortune's part: 'the sun going down like a broken wheel; / and everything at my back'. The poems create an unreliable landscape in which only the sea can be depended upon to be itself (and is brilliantly written about – 'the sea gone white / as if water could run under frost'; the simple beauty of that idea stops one in one's tracks). Nothing is steadfast, and the sky is prone to strange exhibitions of colour: '. . . do whatever you must, so long as that purple-and-yellow blush / in the sky doesn't mean what it seems . . .'

There are many roads – more and less travelled. Night overwhelms day. In 'The Garden Hammock', night advances with startling speed to cancel out a summer scene. All the garden poems are wonderful and strange. The houses in this landscape haunt themselves. Rain is always on the cards. And the cards, when consulted, augur badly. There are many dawns, most of them false.

The poems pursue a solitary journey in which a woman is sometimes sighted but unreachable, as if seen from another world: 'A woman is laying a table; the cloth / billows as it settles; a wineglass catches the light.' But these poems do not need personal effects, names, faces, birthmarks. Harsent has a dreamer's eye and an unerring ear. He has a gift for finding last lines that know they must be the last. 'Vanitas' ends with an ostensible irresolution that turns out to be conclusive: 'what happens next is anybody's guess: / the window a mirror perhaps, the room a wilderness'. One wants to speak this aloud for the pleasure of its final rhyme – the way the three syllables in wilderness extend themselves so that one can lose oneself in the word.

'Elsewhere', the long poem that ends the collection, is Harsent's most dazzling achievement. 'Elsewhere' might be the title of the entire collection in that it extends the exploration of what it is to be transplanted, on the run. This poem deepens the theme of dispossession, the days and nights of reckoning, the consideration of what it might mean to lose everything. Harsent alludes to loss in so many ways but his poems are treasures – all gain.

The Garden Hammock

Your book is *Summer* by Edith Wharton. A smell
off the borders of something becoming inedible.
Between sleeping and waking, almost nothing at all.
There's music in this, there would have to be: a swell
of strings and bells becoming inaudible,
note by note, before you latch on to it. The girl
in the story won't prosper, that's easy enough to tell.
How did night come on like that? The sky is full
of birds, wingbeats in darkness becoming indelible.

BIBLIOGRAPHY

Poetry

TONIGHT'S LOVER (The *Review*, 1968)
A VIOLENT COUNTRY (Oxford University Press, 1969)
TRUCE (Sycamore Press, 1973)
AFTER DARK (Oxford University Press, 1973)
DREAMS OF THE DEAD (Oxford University Press, 1977)
MISTER PUNCH (Oxford University Press, 1984)
SELECTED POEMS (Oxford University Press, 1989)
STORYBOOK HERO (Sycamore Press, 1992)
NEWS FROM THE FRONT (Oxford University Press, 1993)
THE POTTED PRIEST (Four Seasons Press / Snickersee, 1997)
THE SORROW OF SARAJEVO: VERSIONS OF GORAN SIMIĆ (Cargo Press, 1996)
SPRINTING FROM THE GRAVEYARD: VERSIONS OF GORAN SIMIĆ
    (Oxford University Press, 1997)
A BIRD'S IDEA OF FLIGHT (Faber & Faber, 1998)
MARRIAGE (Faber & Faber, 2002)
LEGION (Faber & Faber, 2005)
SELECTED POEMS 1969-2005 (Faber & Faber, 2007)
NIGHT (Faber & Faber, 2011)
IN SECRET: VERSIONS OF YANNIS RITSOS (Enitharmon, 2012)
SONGS FROM THE SAME EARTH (Rack Press, 2013)
FIRE SONGS (Faber & Faber, 2014)
SALT (Faber & Faber, 2017)

As editor

SAVREMENA BRITANSKA POEZIJA (Sarajevo Writers Union, 1988)
ANOTHER ROUND AT THE PILLARS (Cargo Press, 1999)
RAISING THE IRON (Cargo Press, 2004)

Fiction (as David Harsent)

FROM AN INLAND SEA (Viking / Penguin, 1985)

Fiction (as Jack Curtis)

CROW'S PARLIAMENT (Corgi, 1987)
GLORY (Bantam Press, 1989)
SONS OF THE MORNING (Bantam Press, 1991)
POINT OF IMPACT (Bantam Press, 1991)
CONJURE ME (Bantam Press, 1992)
THE CONFESSOR (Orion, 1997)

Fiction (as David Lawrence)

CIRCLE OF THE DEAD/THE DEAD SIT ROUND IN A RING (Thomas Dunne
   Books, 2002)
NOTHING LIKE THE NIGHT (Michael Joseph, 2003)
COLD KILL (Michael Joseph, 2005)
DOWN INTO DARKNESS (Michael Joseph, 2007)

Drama

JENNY GREENTEETH (*The Next Review*, 2015)

Words for music

SERENADE THE SELKIE (music by Julian Grant)
WHEN SHE DIED (music by Jonathan Dove)
CRIME FICTION (music by Huw Watkins)
IN THE LOCKED ROOM (music by Huw Watkins)
GAWAIN (music by Harrison Birtwistle)
THE WOMAN AND THE HARE (music by Harrison Birtwistle)
THE RING DANCE OF THE NAZARENE (music by Harrison Birtwistle)
THE MINOTAUR (music by Harrison Birtwistle)
THE CORRIDOR (music by Harrison Birtwistle)
THE CURE (music by Harrison Birtwistle)
SONGS FROM THE SAME EARTH (music by Harrison Birtwistle)
THE JUDAS PASSION (music by Sally Beamish)

NOTES ON CONTRIBUTORS

SALLY BEAMISH was born in London. Also a viola player and pianist, she moved to Scotland in 1990 to focus on composition. She has won Royal Philharmonic Society and Paul Hamlyn Awards, and in 2012 and 2015 was BBC Radio 3 Composer of the Week. Her ballet *The Tempest*, with Birmingham Royal Ballet and choreographer David Bintley, was premiered in Birmingham, at Sadler's Wells and in Houston, USA in 2016; a year which also saw three piano concerto premieres: for Ronald Brautigam, Martin Roscoe and Jonathan Biss. Her second ballet, *The Little Mermaid*, for Northern Ballet, with choreographer David Nixon, toured Britain in 2017/18. *The Judas Passion*, with librettist David Harsent, was premiered in the UK in 2017 by the Orchestra of the Age of Enlightenment, and then in San Francisco by Philharmonia Baroque. She performs regularly as violist, pianist and narrator. She is currently composer-in-residence with the Academy of St Martin-in-the Fields.

FIONA BENSON first read David Harsent's work in her local bookshop in 2005; she flipped open *Legion* and had to sit on the floor because it made her feel faint! She has been devoted to his work ever since. She wishes she could emulate his lovely line, and the hallucinatory vividness and viscerality of his image. One of her happiest memories is sitting in his garden with his lovely, grey, orange-eyed cat that thinks it's a dog, on a break from judging the Roehampton Poetry Prize with him. He is one of the kindest people she has ever met, as well as being a fiercely moral, impossibly gifted inspiration.

JOHN BURNSIDE is a writer of fiction and creative non-fiction, and an award-winning poet, whose collection *Black Cat Bone* won both the T. S. Eliot and the Forward Prizes for 2011. He is an occasional contributor to the *London Review of Books* and writes a regular nature column for the *New Statesman*; for the last three years, he has been working on the relationship between chronic insomnia and heavy metal music.

SIR HARRISON BIRTWISTLE CH is one of the leading European figures in contemporary music. He was born in Accrington in 1934 and studied clarinet and composition at the Royal Manchester College of Music alongside contemporaries Peter Maxwell Davies, Alexander Goehr, John Ogdon and Elgar Howarth. In 1960 he sold his clarinets to devote his efforts to composition, and travelled to Princeton as a Harkness Fellow, where he completed the opera *Punch and Judy*, establishing himself as a leading voice in British music. He has received commissions from performing organisations worldwide, and his music has been featured in major festivals and concert series including the BBC Proms, Salzburg, Glyndebourne, Holland and Lucerne Festivals, Stockholm New Music, Wien Modern, Wittener Tage and the Southbank and Barbican Centres. Notable collaborations with David Harsent include operas *Gawain* (1991) and *The Minotaur* (2008) for the Royal Opera, *The Woman and the Hare* (1999) for soprano, reciter and ensemble (1999) and *Songs from the Same Earth* (2013) song cycle for tenor and piano.

JOHN CLEGG works as a bookseller in London. His most recent collection is *Holy Toledo!* (Carcanet, 2017).

STEVEN GROARKE is Professor of Social Thought at the University of Roehampton. He teaches at the Institute of Psychoanalysis in London, is an Honorary Senior Research Associate at University College London, and a training analyst of the Association of Child Psychotherapists. He is a member of the Editorial Board and Reviewing Panel, respectively, of the *International Journal of Psychoanalysis* and the *British Journal of Psychotherapy*. He currently works as a psychoanalyst in private practice in London.

KATE KELLAWAY is poetry editor of the *Observer*.

PATRICK MACKIE lives in Gloucestershire and is the author of *The Further Adventures Of The Lives Of The Saints* (CB Editions, 2016).

ANDRÉ NAFFIS-SAHELY is the author of *The Promised Land: Poems from Itinerant Life* (Penguin, 2017). His translations include twenty titles of fiction, poetry and non-fiction from French and Italian. His latest projects are *The Other Side of Nowhere* (Rough Trade Books, 2019), his first poetry pamphlet, and *The Heart of a Stranger: An Anthology of Exile Literature* (Pushkin Press, 2019).

NICOLA NATHAN was brought up in Wales and lives in the Chilterns. Her poems have been published in magazines including *Poetry London, The Edinburgh Review, Ambit, The High Window* and *Wild Court*. Her pamphlet, *Tiny*, was published by *The Next Review* in September 2016.

SEAN O'BRIEN's ninth collection of poems, *Europa* (2018), was shortlisted for the T. S. Eliot Prize, of which he is a previous winner. His book-length poem *Hammersmith* is due to appear in 2020, as is his collection of essays *Dreams are Licensed as They Never Were*. His verse translation of Lope de Vega's Golden Age comedy *The Sicilian Courtesan* is to be staged this year. In 2017 he was Weidenfeld Visiting Professor of Comparative European Literature at St Anne's College, Oxford. He is Professor of Creative Writing at Newcastle and a Fellow of the Royal Society of Literature. He lives in Newcastle upon Tyne.

RUTH PADEL's most recent poetry collection is *Emerald*, a lyrical exploration of finding value in the mourning process and a celebration of her feisty mother. She was Chair of Judges for the 2016 T. S. Eliot Prize and Judge for the 2016 International Man Booker Prize, is Professor of Poetry at King's College London and Fellow of the Royal Society of Literature. Her next collection will be *Beethoven Variations*, in January 2020.

PATRICK DAVIDSON ROBERTS was born in 1987 and grew up in Sunderland and Durham. He was editor of *The Next Review* magazine from 2013 to 2017, and co-founded Offord Road Books in 2017. He is a contributing editor to the Poetry Archive, and reviews for the Poetry School. His debut collection, *The Mains*, was published in 2018 by Vanguard Editions.

DECLAN RYAN was born in Mayo, Ireland and lives in London. His debut pamphlet was published in the Faber New Poets series in 2014. His essays and reviews have been published in the *TLS*, *New Statesman*, *LARB*, *The Believer*, *Boxing News* and elsewhere. A new pamphlet, *Fighters, Losers*, was published in May 2019.

RICHARD SCOTT was born in London in 1981. His pamphlet *Wound* (Rialto, 2016) won the Michael Marks Poetry Award and his poem 'crocodile' won the 2017 Poetry London Competition. *Soho* (Faber, 2018) is his first book and was shortlisted for the T. S. Eliot Prize. He teaches poetry at the Faber Academy.

LAVINIA SINGER worked at Enitharmon Press from 2013 to 2016. She is currently the Assistant Editor, Poetry at Faber & Faber. Her writing has been published in a variety of magazines, journals and anthologies.

FREDERICK TAYLOR grew up in Aylesbury, Buckinghamshire. He read History and Languages at Oxford and in the 1970s travelled widely in Germany, East and West. He now works as a freelance writer whose books include *Dresden* and *The Berlin Wall* (Bloomsbury). He lives in Cornwall with the poet Alice Kavounas.

HUGO WILLIAMS was born in 1942 and grew up in Sussex. He worked on *The London Magazine* from 1961 to 1970, since when he has earned his living as a journalist and travel writer. *Billy's Rain* won the T. S. Eliot Prize in 1999, and *I Knew the Bride* (2014) was shortlisted for the Forward and the T. S. Eliot prizes. His *Collected Poems* was published in 2002, and in 2004 he received the Queen's Gold Medal for Poetry. His most recent collection is *Lines Off* (Faber, 2019).

ACKNOWLEDGEMENTS

The editors are grateful to all the authors for their thoughtful and generous contributions. They are also thankful to those publications who kindly gave their permission to republish a number of pieces in this festschrift.

Portrait photograph of David Harsent reproduced early in this book is by Simon Harsent, © 2014.

In respect of the Foreword, Matthew Hollis would like to acknowledge the scholarship of Jonathan Barnes, Brooks Haxton and Leonardo Taran.

Extract from *The Judas Passion* by Sally Beamish, libretto by David Harsent © 2017 reproduced by kind permission of Peters Edition, London.

Essay 'Back to Princes Risborough' by Hugo Williams was originally published in Williams's long-running 'Freelance' column, which began in 1988 in the *Times Literary Supplement*. This piece appeared in 2007.

Review of *Night* by Kate Kellaway was first published in the *Guardian* on 13th February 2011 and syndicated from Guardian News and Media. The poem that accompanies it, 'The Garden Hammock', by David Harsent, is printed with the permission of Faber & Faber.

Essay 'You Thought Love Owed You Everything' by André Naffis-Sahely was first published in *The Paris Review* on 25th September 2015.